Getting Started with SOQL

Revolutionize the use of simple query strings
to make them more efficient using SOQL

Magulan D

[PACKT] PUBLISHING open source community experience distilled

BIRMINGHAM - MUMBAI

Getting Started with SOQL

First published: April 2014

Production Reference: 1090414

Published by Packt Publishing Ltd.
Livery Place
35 Livery Street
Birmingham B3 2PB, UK.

ISBN 978-1-78328-735-2

www.packtpub.com

Cover Image by Neha Rajappan (neha.rajappan1@gmail.com)

Credits

Author
Magulan D

Reviewers
Satheesh Kumar A
Carlos Ernesto Descalzi
David W. Grigsby
Lisha Murthy
Vinayendra Nataraja

Acquisition Editors
Joanne Fitzpatrick
Antony Lowe

Content Development Editor
Nadeem N. Bagban

Technical Editor
Novina Kewalramani

Copy Editors
Dipti Kapadia
Aditya Nair
Stuti Srivastava

Project Coordinator
Harshal Ved

Proofreader
Maria Gould

Indexer
Hemangini Bari

Production Coordinator
Conidon Miranda

Cover Work
Conidon Miranda

About the Author

Magulan D is a Salesforce.com administrator and developer. He started his career as a PHP developer and also worked as a Siebel CRM developer. During his career as a PHP developer, he created many sites.

Magulan is also a blogger, posting many useful tutorials relating to Salesforce.com development and administration works. Often these are workarounds for problems or issues that people usually face in their development. He has been working as a Salesforce.com developer since 2011.

First and foremost, I would like to thank Packt Publishing for giving me the opportunity to write this book. I would like to thank Joanne and Harshal for their continuous support in publishing this book.

I would like to thank Satheesh Kumar for his continuous effort in reviewing the book in spite of his busy schedule. He supported and encouraged me throughout my writing.

I would like to thank my wife Gowripriya for her support and motivation. She helped me a lot in my writing. She motivated me to write this book. Her reviews and comments helped me complete my writing. It was a long and difficult journey for her. I dedicate this book to her.

I would like to express my gratitude to all the people in Packt Publishing who supported me in publishing this book.

About the Reviewers

Satheesh Kumar A is a 24-year-old software professional from India. After completing his degree in Engineering, Satheesh selected his profession as a software developer with one of the most reputed IT service providers in India. Satheesh started his career as a Force.com developer, and he is now comfortable with all the forms of application development and administration in Force.com.

Carlos Ernesto Descalzi is a system developer with 15 years of experience, working mostly in different Java technologies, from JEE to Swing, JNI, developing from web applications to distributed and embedded systems.

Carlos is currently working with the G&L Group, and has been since 2007. He has been working as a Force.com developer for the last year. He worked as a JEE developer until then.

Other past companies where he has worked include the following:

- An independent consultant (2006-2007) as a JEE developer
- Snoop Consulting (2005-2006) as a JEE developer
- Idea Factory Software (2004-2005) as a JEE developer
- NEC Argentina (2001-2004) as a developer of biometric and security systems using embedded technologies

Special thanks to my wife Dalila.

David W. Grigsby is currently focused on the integration of the Software as a Service (SaaS) application between on-premise and cloud applications using DocuSign to extend Salesforce, Google, and others to streamline virtual offices and remote personnel and increase the revenue production and marketing reach using new media technologies such as LinkedIn, Facebook, and Twitter.

His experience in development ranges from embedded devices, which generally use C++ and assembly language, to PCs that use the major PC languages and .NET. He has worked in the object-oriented development space since Visual C++ with MFC and Visual Foxpro 3.0 have been in the market. Microsoft Visual Studio and the .NET framework are continued extensions of this experience.

In all, he brings more than 30 years of business experience in broad systems, development, and whatever project he has been involved with.

His specialties are development languages, Microsoft Visual Studio, .NET, SQL, Consulting, Program Manager, Microsoft ISV, Microsoft Partner, Embedded Devices, instrumentation and debugging, architecture design for enterprise environments, Novell CNE, and Microsoft MCSE.

He loves his family and friends, the outdoors, art and music, learning new technologies, and pushing the envelope.

His past employers include Grigsby Consulting LLC, Microsoft, and DocuSign.

He has worked on the following books:

- *How to send a DocuSign™ envelope via REST in 10 minutes: A developer lab from Grigsby Consulting LLC's Integration Cookbook Volume 2* [Kindle Edition]
- *How to login to DocuSign™ via REST in 10 minutes: A developer lab from Grigsby Consulting LLC's Integration Cookbook Volume 2* [Kindle Edition]
- *How to login to Salesforce™ via SOAP in 10 minutes: A developer lab from Grigsby Consulting LLC's Integration Cookbook Volume 2* [Kindle Edition]
- *How to get a DocuSign™ template via SOAP in 10 minutes: A developer lab from Grigsby Consulting LLC's Integration Cookbook Volume 2* [Kindle Edition]

Vinayendra Nataraja is a developer and an information security enthusiast. He has worked on Salesforce as a developer for almost 3 years. He is a member of the Information System Security Association. Vinayendra is a passionate, self-driven individual who has won awards and accolades for his work. In his spare time, he finds security bugs and has won bug bounties for this. He is known as the "Bug Hunter" among his friends.

Vinayendra started his career as an application developer at Akamai Technologies, India. He then interned at Salesforce, USA in the summer of 2013 as a Tools and Automation Intern. He is currently working with Northeastern University as a Salesforce developer. He will be joining Salesforce.com as a Product Security Engineer this summer.

Vinayendra is currently pursuing a Master of Science degree in Information Assurance at Northeastern University, Boston, USA. He completed his undergraduate degree in Computer Science from Rashtreeya Vidyalaya College of Engineering, Bangalore, India.

Reviewing this book was a great experience. I would like to thank the author and the publisher for presenting this opportunity to me. This book is a gift to developers who have just started learning Salesforce, as it provides a solid foundation with concepts explained in a simple language.

---

www.PacktPub.com

Support files, eBooks, discount offers and more

You might want to visit www.PacktPub.com for support files and downloads related to your book.

Did you know that Packt offers eBook versions of every book published, with PDF and ePub files available? You can upgrade to the eBook version at www.PacktPub.com and as a print book customer, you are entitled to a discount on the eBook copy. Get in touch with us at service@packtpub.com for more details.

PACKT LIB

http://PacktLib.PacktPub.com

Do you need instant solutions to your IT questions? PacktLib is Packt's online digital book library. Here, you can access, read and search across Packt's entire library of books.

Why Subscribe?

- Fully searchable across every book published by Packt
- Copy and paste, print and bookmark content
- On demand and accessible via web browser

Free Access for Packt account holders

If you have an account with Packt at www.PacktPub.com, you can use this to access PacktLib today and view nine entirely free books. Simply use your login credentials for immediate access.

Table of Contents

Preface	**1**
Chapter 1: Introduction to SOQL	**5**
What is SOQL?	**5**
Purpose of SOQL	**8**
SOQL syntax	**9**
Writing your first SOQL statement	**13**
Summary	**24**
Chapter 2: Basic SOQL Statements	**25**
The alias notation	**25**
The WHERE clause	**27**
The comparison operators	**29**
The equals operator	30
The not equals operator	30
The less than or equal to operator	32
The less than operator	32
The greater than or equal to operator	33
The greater than operator	34
The LIKE operator	36
The IN operator	**37**
The NOT IN operator	37
The logical operators	**39**
The AND operator	39
The OR operator	39
The ORDER BY clause	**41**
The INCLUDES and EXCLUDES operators	**43**
Summary	**44**

Chapter 3: Advanced SOQL Statements **45**
Relationship queries **45**
Filtering multiselect picklist values **50**
The INCLUDES operator 50
The EXCLUDES operator 52
The escape sequences **53**
The date formats **54**
The date literals **54**
Querying with the date fields **57**
Sorting in both the ascending and descending orders **58**
Using the GROUP BY ROLLUP clause **59**
Using the FOR REFERENCE clause **60**
Using the FOR VIEW clause **60**
Using the GROUP BY CUBE clause **61**
Using the OFFSET clause **62**
Summary **63**
Chapter 4: Functions in SOQL **65**
Using the toLabel() method **65**
Using the GROUP BY clause **67**
Using the COUNT() method **68**
Using the COUNT(Field_Name) method **69**
Using the COUNT_DISTINCT() method **70**
Using the MIN() method **71**
Using the MAX() method **72**
Using the SUM() method **73**
Using the HAVING clause **74**
Summary **75**
Chapter 5: Limitations and Best Practices **77**
Standards to be followed in SOQL **77**
Best practices **78**
Limitations in objects **79**
Other limitations **80**
Governor limits 80
Understanding the limitations of the ORDER BY query 81
Understanding the limitations of the toLabel() query 81
Understanding the limitations of the COUNT() query 82
Understanding the limitations of the OFFSET clause 82
Limitations of the relationship queries 82
Notes and Attachments limitations 83
Summary **83**

Chapter 6: Tools with Installation Guidelines **85**
Using the Force.com Explorer software **85**
Installing Force.com Explorer 85
Workbench **89**
Dataloader.io **93**
The Apex Data Loader tool **97**
Downloading Data Loader without the Salesforce.com login 100
Summary **104**
Appendix: Review Questions **105**
Index **111**

Preface

SOQL plays a vital role in the development of Salesforce.com and administration tasks. As a developer or as an administrator in Salesforce.com, we write many SOQL statements to fetch and validate the data present in the objects. If we know all the features in SOQL, we can easily write optimized SOQL statements to filter the data and fetch the required data from the object.

The sample queries used in this book will help you to understand the SOQL features easily. In the first few chapters, the sample queries are intended for beginners and for developers or administrators who are new to Salesforce.com. In the rest of the chapters, the sample queries are intended for Salesforce.com experts. So, in the first part, simple queries are used, and in the next part, complex queries are used for an easier understanding of the SOQL features. Real-time examples are used as sample queries. These examples include querying data from a single object as well as querying data from multiple objects in a single query.

This book also addresses the standards and guidelines to be followed when writing SOQL statements. The standards and guidelines discussed in this book will help you to write SOQL statements without hitting any limitation set by Salesforce.com and to avoid unwanted data fetched through the queries.

The last chapter provides the installation procedures to be followed to install the software needed to execute SOQL statements. These software help us to get the real-time data from the objects for viewing. They also help you to execute the sample queries used in this book in each and every chapter simultaneously.

The most interesting part is the knowledge check at the end of each chapter. The knowledge check is a kind of assessment that grabs our attention and concentration and helps us to recollect the topics learnt in that chapter. It is also helpful for Salesforce.com certification preparation.

What this book covers

Chapter 1, Introduction to SOQL, shows what SOQL is and its purpose. While discussing its purpose, we will see where exactly we should use SOQL statements in Salesforce.com development and administration.

Chapter 2, Basic SOQL Statements, shows how to write basic SOQL statements in Salesforce.com. We will start with simple alias notation. We will try out many examples to differentiate objects using alias notation.

Chapter 3, Advanced SOQL Statements, shows how to query records from more than one object using relationship queries. The steps to get the relationship name among objects will also be provided.

Chapter 4, Functions in SOQL, shows all the functions that are available in SOQL. It discusses about the methods for translating the field values using toLabel(), which will be very useful when we want to translate the values and show them in a report.

Chapter 5, Limitations and Best Practices, shows the standards to be followed when writing SOQL statements. The best practice explained here allows us to retrieve the required records by filtering well. As a developer or as an administrator, we should follow these standards and best practices.

Chapter 6, Tools with Installation Guidelines, shows a few tools that are available to execute SOQL statements. The installation guidelines will also be discussed with step-by-step instructions.

What you need for this book

A basic knowledge in Salesforce.com CRM is a prerequisite to follow the examples in this book. A basic knowledge of SQL is an added advantage.

Who this book is for

This book is intended for Salesforce.com developers and administrators. Developers and administrators with a basic knowledge of Salesforce.com will find the material in this book accessible without additional preparation. Salesforce.com developers and administrators will find all the features that are available for writing SOQL statements.

Conventions

In this book, you will find a number of styles of text that distinguish between different kinds of information. Here are some examples of these styles, and an explanation of their meaning.

Code words in text, database table names, folder names, filenames, file extensions, pathnames, dummy URLs, user input, and Twitter handles are shown as follows:

"Filtering a multiselect picklist field using the `INCLUDES` and `EXCLUDES` operators will be discussed in detail."

Any command-line input or output is written as follows:

```
SELECT Id, Name FROM Account
```

New terms and **important words** are shown in bold. Words that you see on the screen, in menus or dialog boxes for example, appear in the text like this: "The **Objects** link displays all the custom objects available in our organization."

> Warnings or important notes appear in a box like this.

> Tips and tricks appear like this.

Reader feedback

Feedback from our readers is always welcome. Let us know what you think about this book—what you liked or may have disliked. Reader feedback is important for us to develop titles that you really get the most out of.

To send us general feedback, simply send an e-mail to `feedback@packtpub.com`, and mention the book title via the subject of your message.

If there is a topic that you have expertise in and you are interested in either writing or contributing to a book, see our author guide on `www.packtpub.com/authors`.

Customer support

Now that you are the proud owner of a Packt book, we have a number of things to help you to get the most from your purchase.

Errata

an error in printing or writing

Although we have taken every care to ensure the accuracy of our content, mistakes do happen. If you find a mistake in one of our books—maybe a mistake in the text or the code—we would be grateful if you would report this to us. By doing so, you can save other readers from frustration and help us improve subsequent versions of this book. If you find any errata, please report them by visiting `http://www.packtpub.com/submit-errata`, selecting your book, clicking on the **errata submission form** link, and entering the details of your errata. Once your errata are verified, your submission will be accepted and the errata will be uploaded on our website, or added to any list of existing errata, under the Errata section of that title. Any existing errata can be viewed by selecting your title from `http://www.packtpub.com/support`.

Piracy

Piracy of copyright material on the Internet is an ongoing problem across all media. At Packt, we take the protection of our copyright and licenses very seriously. If you come across any illegal copies of our works, in any form, on the Internet, please provide us with the location address or website name immediately so that we can pursue a remedy.

Please contact us at `copyright@packtpub.com` with a link to the suspected pirated material.

We appreciate your help in protecting our authors, and our ability to bring you valuable content.

Questions

You can contact us at `questions@packtpub.com` if you are having a problem with any aspect of the book, and we will do our best to address it.

1
Introduction to SOQL

You will be introduced to SOQL in this chapter. This chapter will also discuss the API names of standard objects, custom objects, standard fields, and custom fields. These API names are used while querying using SOQL statements. This chapter explains when and where we use SOQL statements in Salesforce.

SOQL syntax will give us more information, such as reserved keywords in SOQL, how to write SOQL statements, and so on. We will get started by writing our first SOQL statement in this chapter.

What is SOQL?

Salesforce Object Query Language (**SOQL**) is used to build queries for fetching data in the Force.com platform. Just as we write a query in **Structured Query Language** (**SQL**) with some columns and a table, here, in SOQL, we write a query with some fields and an object. However, SOQL does not support all the features of SQL. For example, the `*` character in the `SELECT` statement denotes all columns in a table in SQL, but it cannot be used in the `SELECT` statement in SOQL. So, to retrieve all fields in SOQL, we have to mention all the fields separated by commas.

SOQL is case insensitive. For ease of use, we suggest you to maintain SOQL keywords in uppercase and fields in initial case (first letter in uppercase and the rest in lowercase). Throughout this book, all SOQL keywords will be written in uppercase and object names, field lists, conditions, and so on will be written in lowercase.

SOQL is very easy to understand if you have prior knowledge in SQL. As mentioned earlier, however, it does not support all the features available in SQL. If we think of tables as objects and columns as fields in Salesforce, writing SOQL becomes easier. Salesforce has standard objects (objects defined by Salesforce) and custom objects (objects defined by the user). The custom object ends with `__c` for identification purposes.

Good knowledge of SOQL helps us to optimize our code. If we are looking for data from different objects, SOQL helps us a lot in accomplishing that. Instead of writing complex code to achieve this, an administrator or developer with vast knowledge of SOQL may easily accomplish these kinds of tasks. The functions available in SOQL reduce our workload and save time.

The sample queries used in this book are real-time examples with step-by-step explanations. Beginners will gain confidence as we go ahead. Administrators and developers can also get ideas on how to optimize their code for faster execution of queries. An administrator can easily build any kind of complex report in an Excel file by extracting data from the objects using SOQL and delivering it to the clients in a timely manner if he or she has good knowledge of SOQL. SOQL eases the tasks of administrators, who are always looking for data.

A developer also faces many situations where they may have to write SOQL queries in Apex programming. If the developer has wide knowledge of SOQL, they can easily accomplish their task without reiterating again and again to form data for manipulation.

Make use of the tools available at `Salesforce.com` to execute the query instantly to clarify any doubts that arise. Salesforce provides tools, and third-party tools are also available. Steps with installation procedures and guidelines are available in *Chapter 6, Tools with Installation Guidelines*. The Developer Console can also be used for the easier and instant execution of queries.

To use SOQL, we need to know the API name of the objects. To know the API names of the standard objects in Salesforce, visit the following reference link provided by Salesforce:

`http://www.salesforce.com/us/developer/docs/api/Content/sforce_api_objects_list.htm`

Since custom objects are user-defined objects, information about these objects will not be available under **Customize** in the Force.com setup.

> The API names of custom objects always end with `__c`.

The steps to get the API name of the custom objects change from environment to environment. In my organization, it is **Setup** | **Build** | **Create** | **Objects**, as shown in the following screenshot. We can view an object's API name on selecting it.

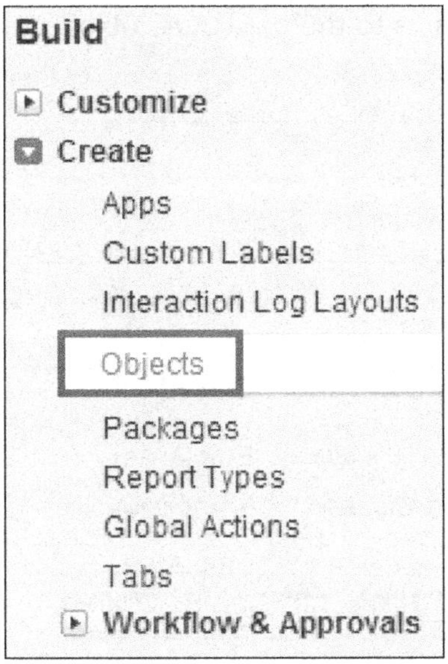

The **Objects** link displays all the custom objects available in our organization, as shown in the following screenshot:

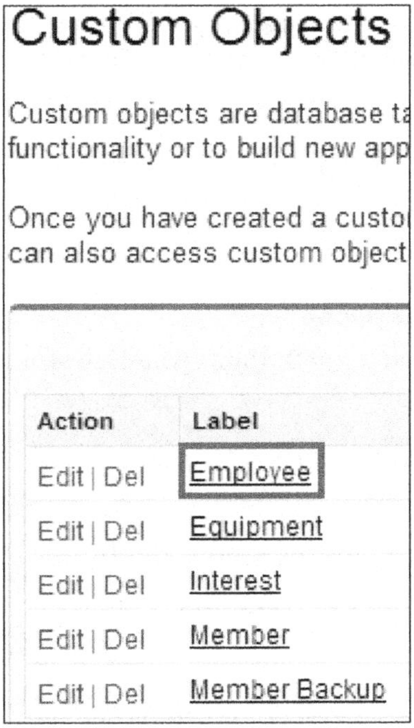

The **Employee** link redirects us to the `Employee` object custom definition, as shown in the following screenshot:

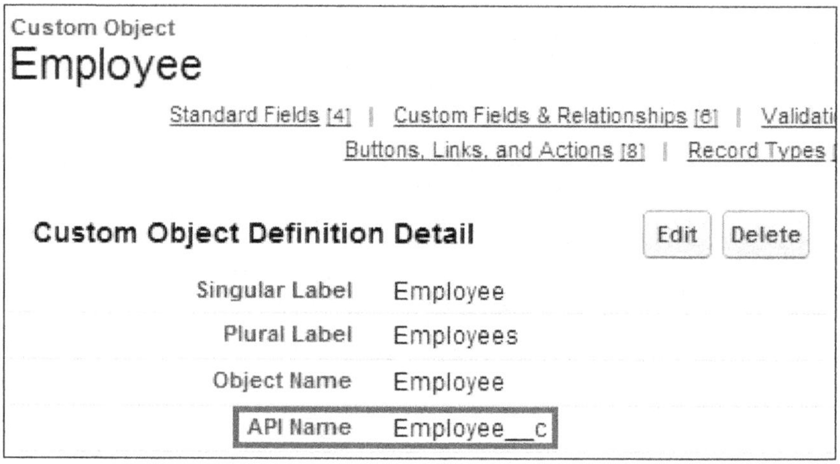

The `SELECT` statement is used to retrieve data from objects. Relationships must exist among objects in case we want to retrieve data from two or more objects.

> It is not possible to write a single SOQL query to fetch records from two objects without any relationship among the two objects in Salesforce.

Relationship queries (queries for fetching records from more than one object) will be discussed in *Chapter 2, Basic SOQL Queries*.

Purpose of SOQL

The main purpose of SOQL is to fetch data from Salesforce objects. SOQL can be used in the following places:

- The `queryString` parameter in the `query()` call
- Apex statements
- Visualforce controllers and the getter methods
- The schema explorer of the Force.com IDE

SOQL syntax

Similar to SQL, SOQL also makes use of the `SELECT` statement to fetch data. Let us explore the following SOQL syntax:

```
SELECT fields
FROM Object
WHERE Condition
Ordering LIMIT
FOR VIEW Or FOR REFERENCE
OFFSET
UPDATE VIEWSTAT
```

The preceding query is explained as follows:

- `fields`: This denotes the API names of the fields of an object
- `Object`: This denotes the custom or standard object
- `Condition`: This is used for filtering records (optional)
- `Ordering`: This is used for ordering the result (optional)
- `Limit`: This is used for limiting the number of fetched records (optional)
- `FOR VIEW`: This updates `LastViewedDate` for fetched records (optional)
- `FOR REFERENCE`: This updates `LastReferencedDate` for fetched records (optional)
- `OFFSET`: This denotes the starting row for fetching (optional)
- `UPDATE VIEWSTAT`: This updates the articles' view statistics for fetched records (optional)

`SELECT`, `fieldList`, `FROM`, and `Object` are required. The others are optional in SOQL.

We should use the API names of the fields in the `SELECT` statement. We should not use the labels of the fields. The API names are available in the object definition. For **Standard Fields**, the **Field Name** column refers to the API name, and for **Custom Fields**, the **API Name** column refers to the API name.

To get the API names of standard objects in Salesforce, navigate to **Setup** | **Build** | **Customize** | **Object** | **Fields**.

> In the Force.com setup, we can get all the information related to standard objects in Salesforce by navigating to **Build** | **Customize**.

Let us see how to get the API names of the `Account` object fields. To get the API names of the `Account` object fields, navigate to **Setup** | **Build** | **Customize** | **Accounts** | **Fields** as shown in the following screenshot. The `Standard` object fields are present under **Customize** and custom objects are present under **Create** | **Objects** in Salesforce.

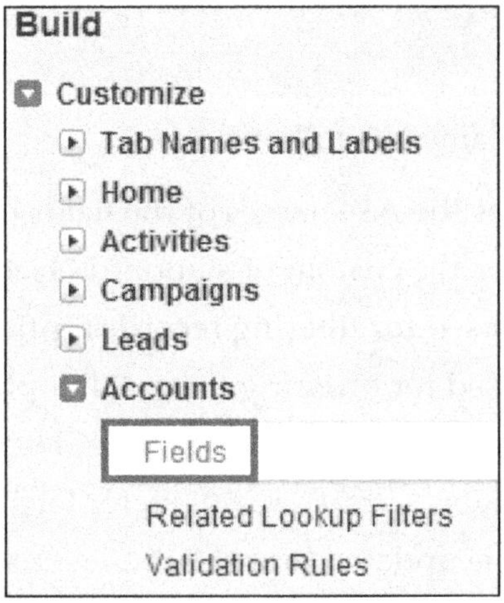

In the **Account Standard Fields** section, the **Field Name** column refers to the API name of the standard fields, as shown in the following screenshot:

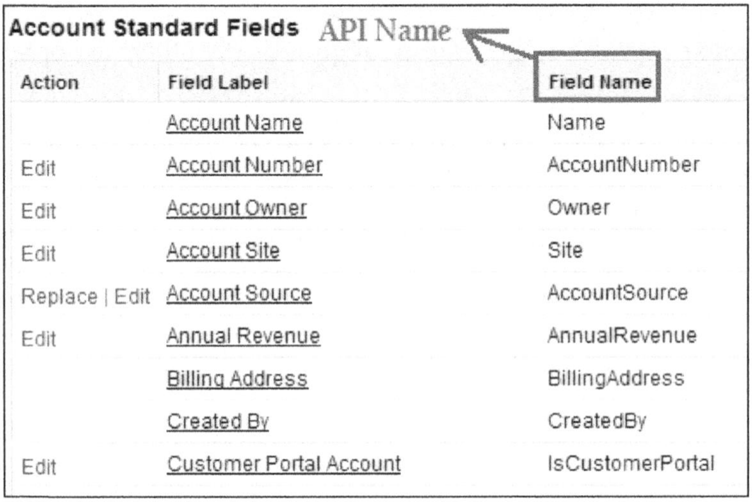

In the **Account Custom Fields & Relationships** section, the **API Name** column denotes the API name of the fields, as shown in the following screenshot:

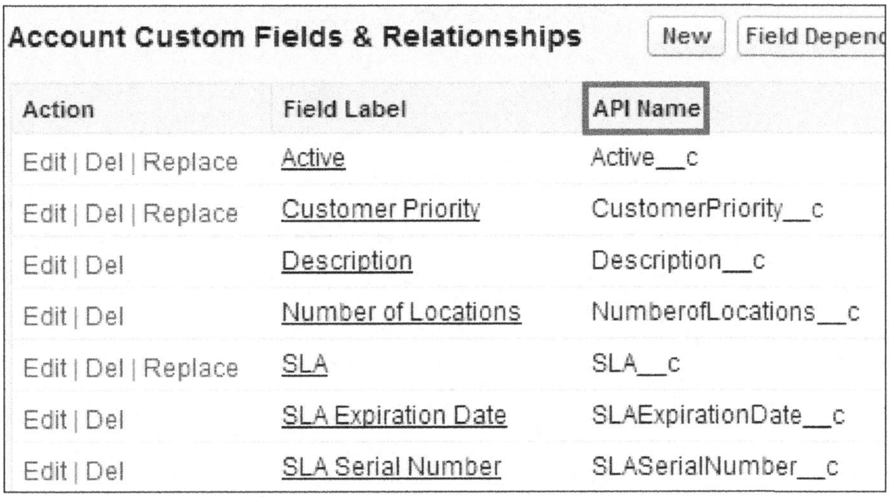

To get the API names of custom objects in Salesforce, navigate to **Setup** | **Build** | **Create** | **Objects**, as shown in the following screenshot, and select the object:

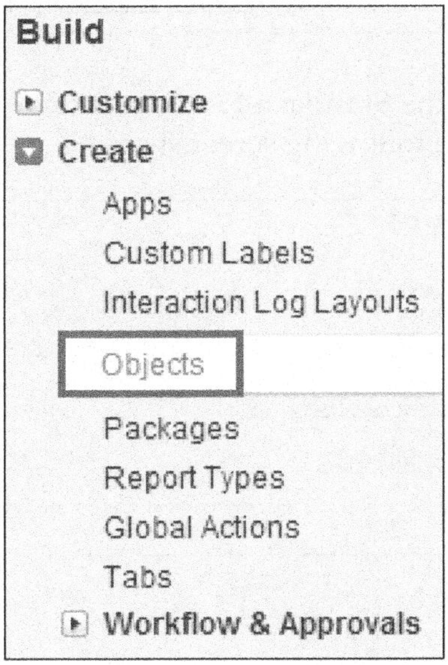

This **Objects** link displays all the custom objects available in our organization, as shown in the following screenshot:

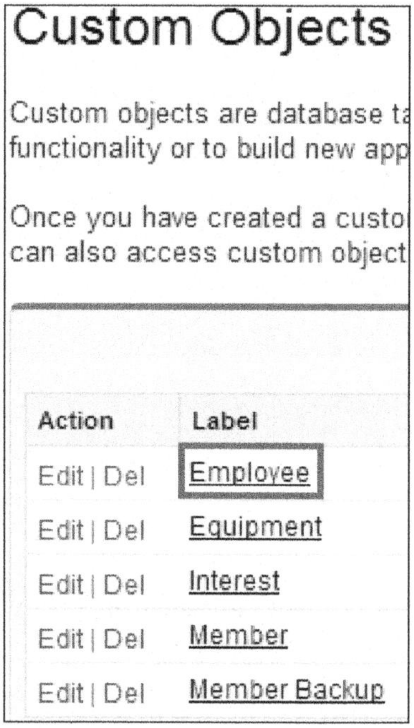

The **Field Name** column in the **Standard Fields** section denotes the API names of the fields, as shown in the following screenshot:

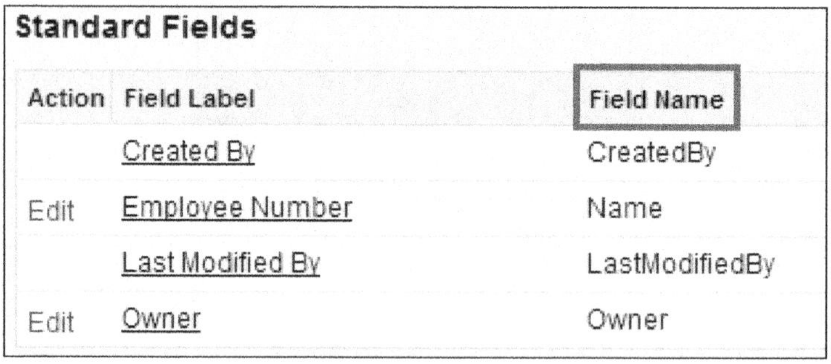

The **API Name** column in the **Custom Fields & Relationships** section denotes the API names of the fields, as shown in the following screenshot:

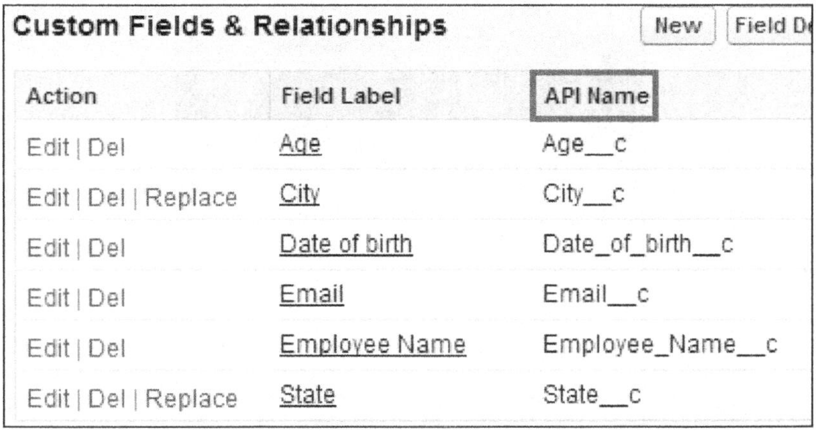

Writing your first SOQL statement

Before getting started with writing our first SOQL statement, we have to install a software to execute our queries. Salesforce offers a couple of tools to write and execute SOQL queries instantly. Salesforce also supports other third-party tools to write and execute queries. Let us write a simple SOQL query to fetch the IDs and names of accounts from the `Account` object.

> `Account` is a standard object in Salesforce. We use the `Account` object to store information about our customers and partners with whom we do business.

A sample query is given as follows:

```
SELECT Id, Name FROM Account
```

Refer to the following screenshot:

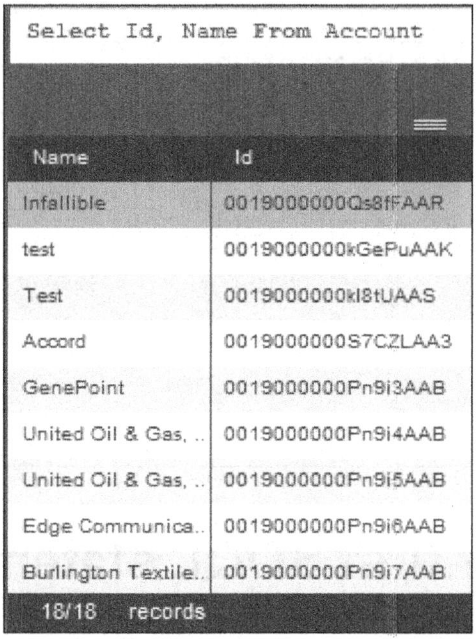

Here, `Id` and `Name` are standard fields of the `Account` object.

> Custom objects and custom fields always end with `__c` in Salesforce.

Let us see another example of how to fetch custom fields in standard objects. Refer to the following screenshot:

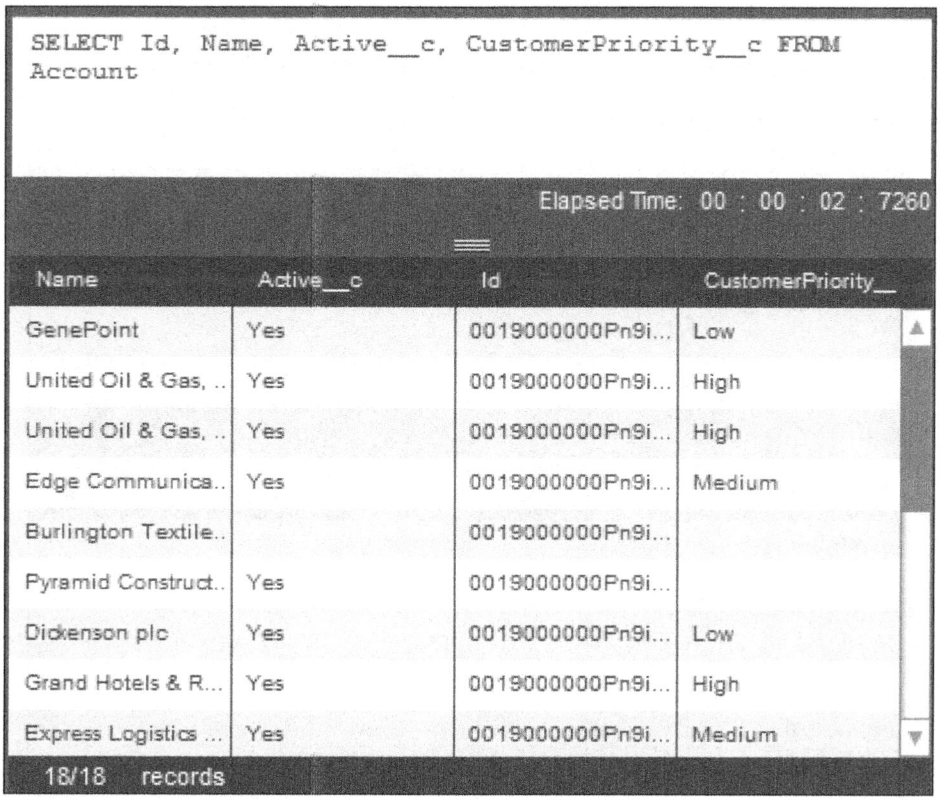

Here, `Id` and `Name` are standard fields and `Active__c` and `CustomerPriority__c` are custom fields.

A sample query is given as follows:

```
SELECT Id, Name, Active__c, CustomerPriority__c FROM Account
```

In the preceding example, we saw how to retrieve records from `Account` (standard object). Let us write a simple SOQL query to fetch records from a custom object. In this example, let us make use of a custom object, `Employee__c`, which has custom fields such as `Employee_Name__c`, `State__c`, `City__c`, and so on.

A sample query is given as follows:

```
SELECT Name, Employee_Name__c, State__c, City__c FROM Employee__c
```

Refer to the following screenshot:

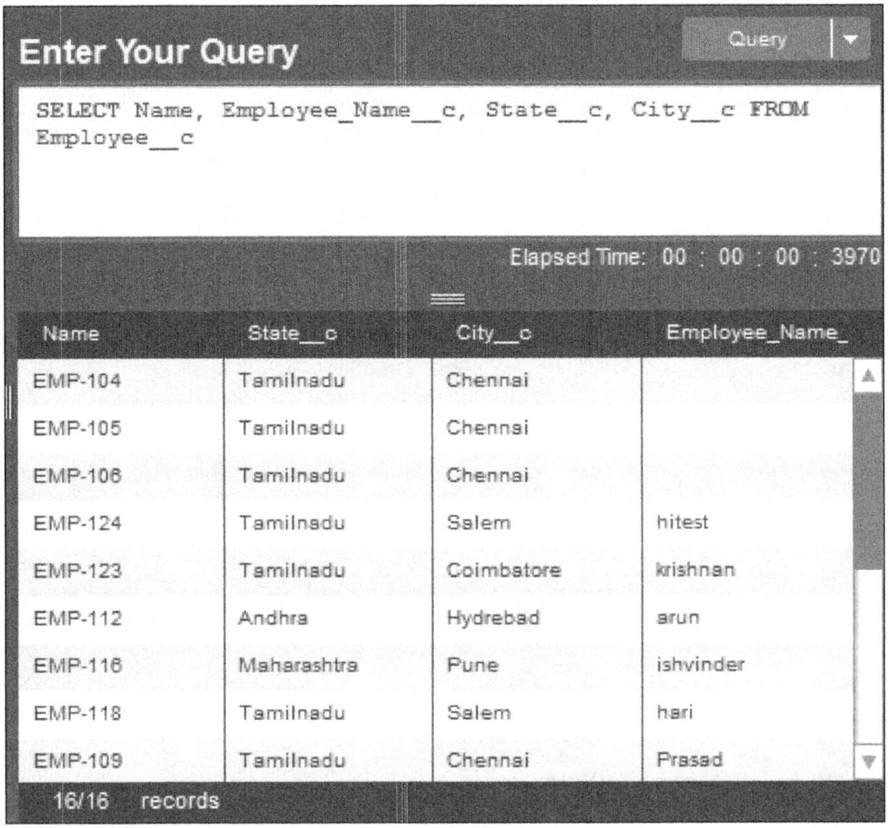

Here, `Employee__c` is a custom object; `Name` is a standard field; and `Employee_Name__c`, `State__c`, and `City__c` are custom fields.

Each and every object in Salesforce has system fields. System fields are read-only fields. The following is a list of system fields:

- `Id`
- `IsDeleted`
- `CreatedById`
- `CreatedDate`

- `LastModifiedById`
- `LastModifiedDate`
- `SystemModstamp`

> All system fields are not editable. Only a few system fields are editable. To get edit access to system fields, we have to contact Salesforce support.

The following table describes field names:

Field Name	Description
`Id`	It is a unique identifier of the record.
`IsDeleted`	It is used to check if the record is in the **Recycle Bin**. If `IsDeleted` is `true`, the record is in the **Recycle Bin**, otherwise the record is not soft deleted.
`CreatedById`	It is the ID of the user who created the record.
`CreatedDate`	It is the date and time this record was created.
`LastModifiedById`	It is the ID of the user who last modified it.
`LastModifiedDate`	It is the date and time this record was last modified by a user.
`SystemModstamp`	It is the date and time when this record was last modified by a user or by an automated process (such as a trigger).

Let us see a sample SOQL query to fetch the system fields:

```
SELECT Id, Name, CreatedDate, LastModifiedDate FROM Account
```

Refer to the following screenshot:

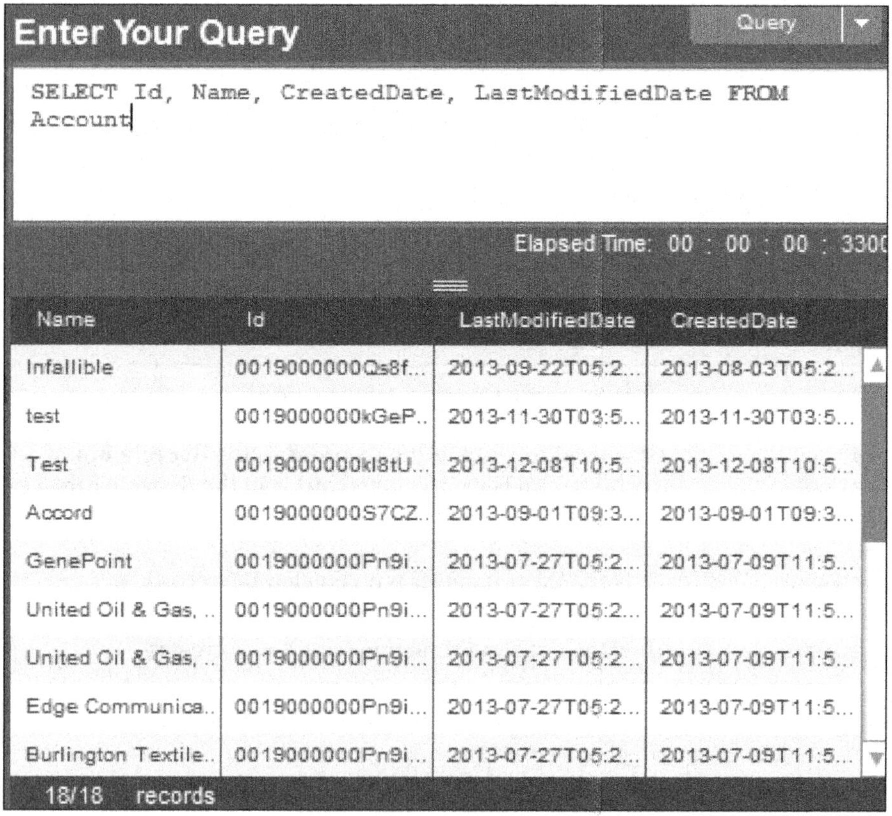

Here, `CreatedDate` and `LastModifiedDate` are system fields.

Let us see another example to fetch `FirstName` and `LastName` from the `User` object.

> The `User` object is also another standard object in Salesforce. The `User` object stores all the information about the users in the organization. The `IsActive` field is used to check whether the user is active or inactive.

A sample query is given as follows:

```
SELECT FirstName, LastName FROM User
```

Refer to the following screenshot:

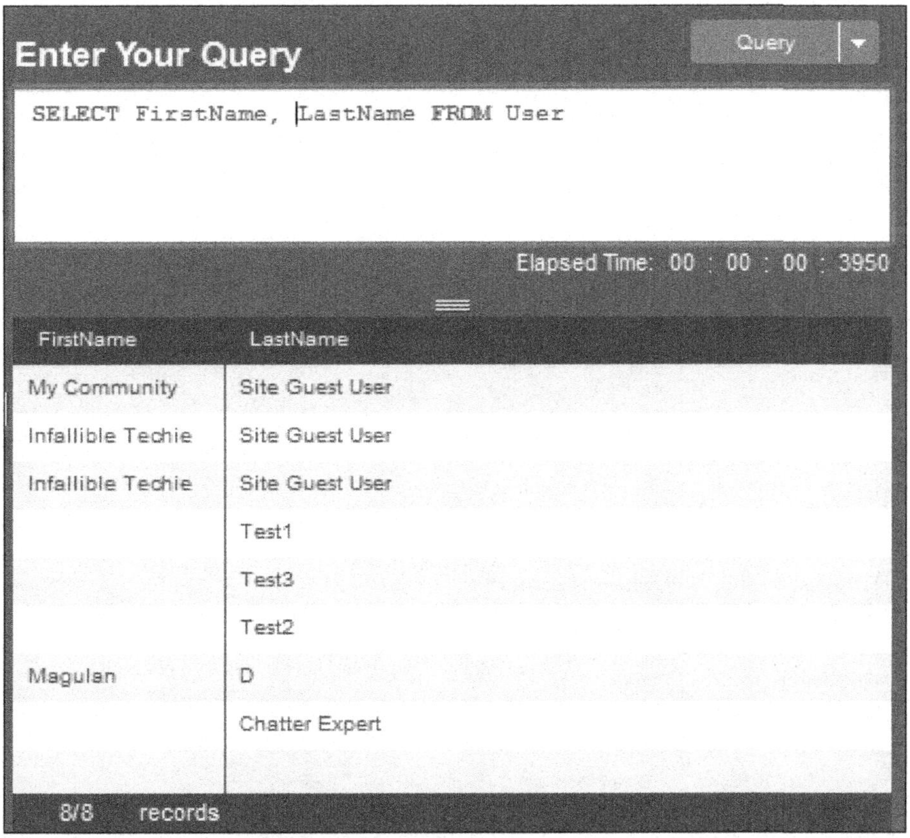

Let us see another example to fetch `Name` and `StageName` from the `Opportunity` object.

> `Opportunity` is an important standard object in the `Sales` application in Salesforce. `Opportunity` is a potential revenue-generating event.

A sample query is given as follows:

```
SELECT Name, StageName FROM Opportunity
```

Refer to the following screenshot:

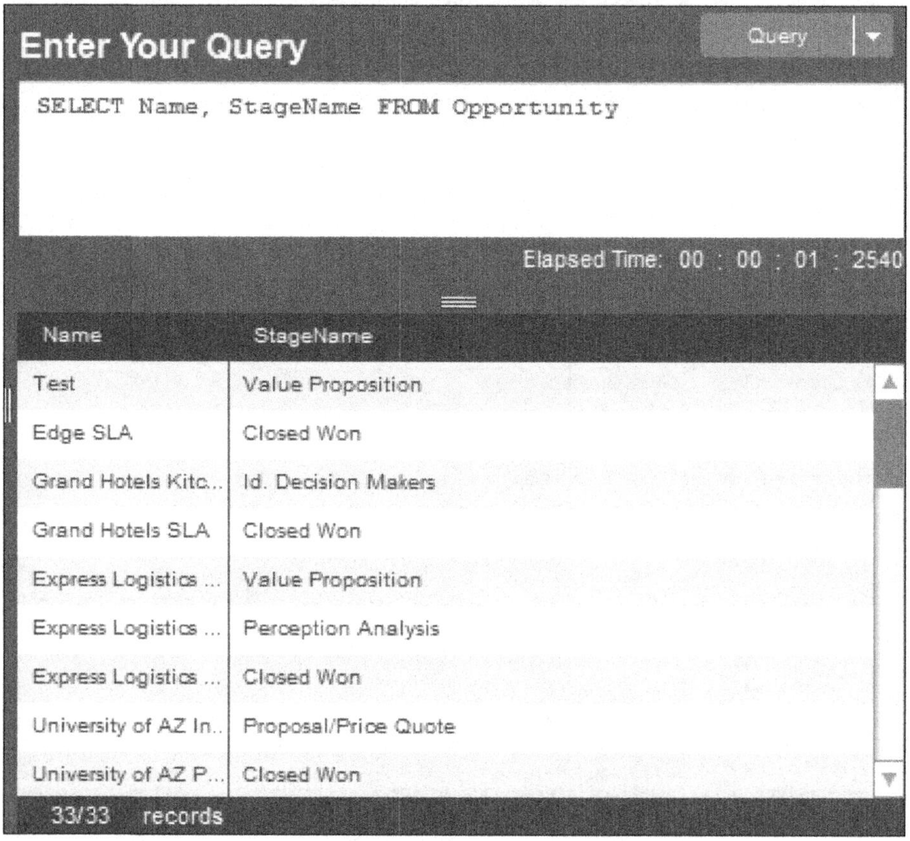

Let us see another example to fetch `Name` and `Status` from the `Lead` object.

> `Lead` is also a standard object in Salesforce. `Lead` is used to store information about an organization or individual persons who are interested in our product. A `Lead` can be converted into a single `Account`, multiple `Contacts`, and multiple `Opportunities` objects.

A sample query is given as follows:

```
SELECT Name, Status FROM Lead
```

Refer to the following screenshot:

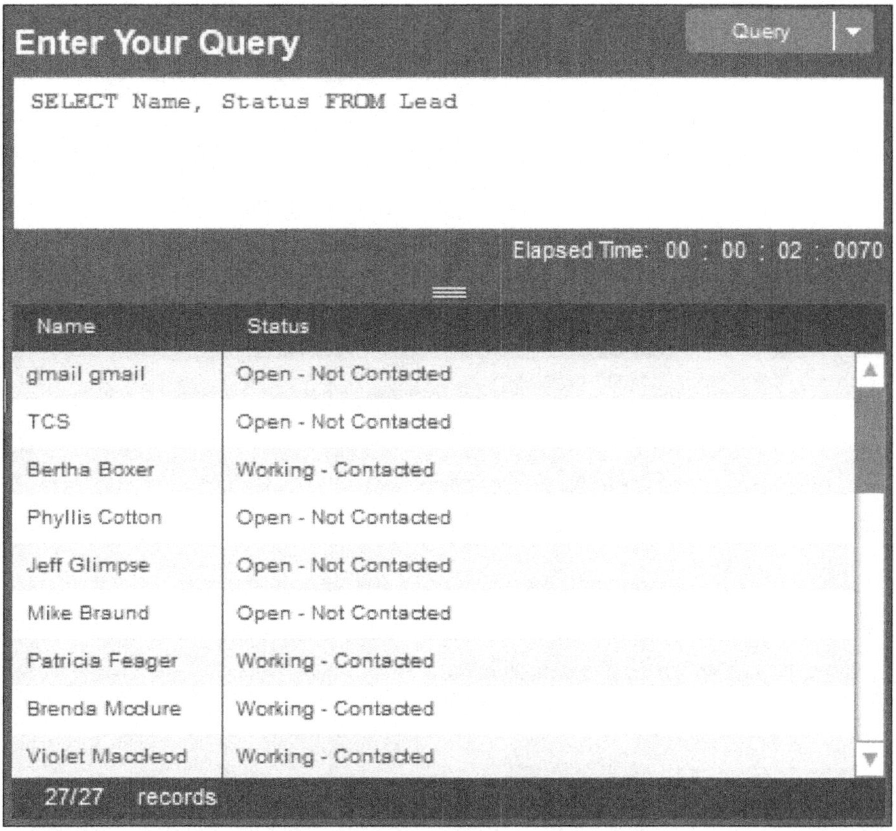

Let us see another example to fetch `Id` and `Name` from the `Product` object. The API name of the `Product` object is `Product2`.

> The `Product2` object stores all the information about the products available in our organization.

A sample query is given as follows:

```
SELECT Id, Name FROM Product2
```

Refer to the following screenshot:

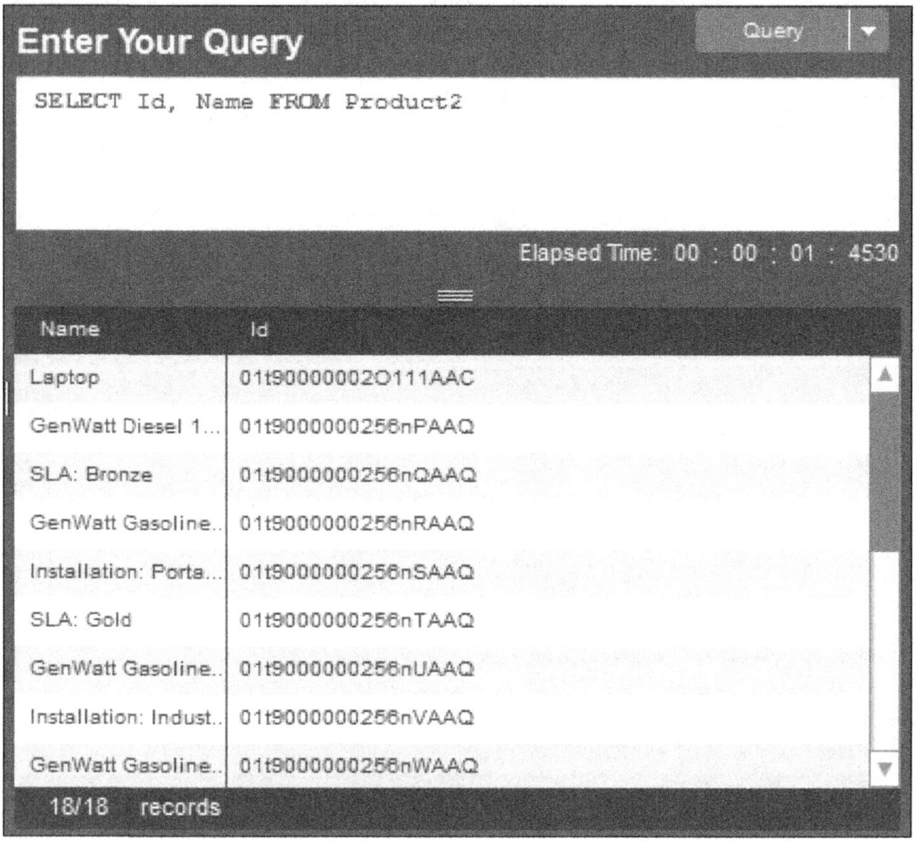

Let us see another example to fetch `Id` and `Name` from the `Price Book` object. The API name of the `Price Book` object is `Pricebook2`.

> `Pricebook2` is another standard object in Salesforce. In the `Pricebook2` object, we use stored information on the different prices of products.

A sample query is given as follows:

```
SELECT Id, Name FROM Pricebook2
```

Refer to the following screenshot:

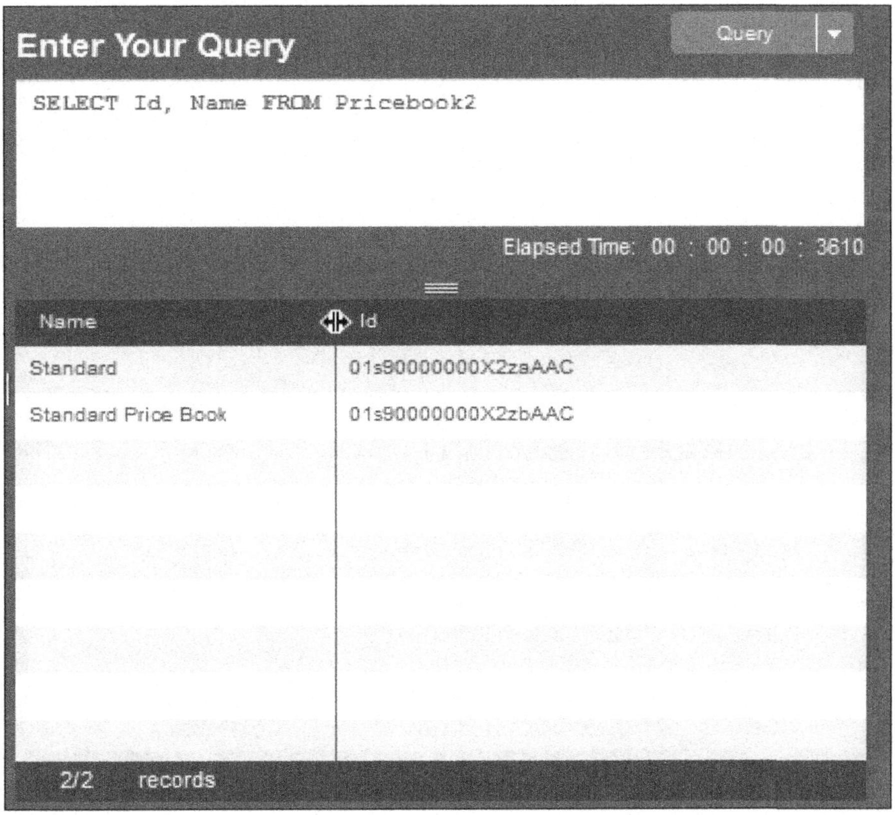

Let us see another example to fetch `ProductCode`, `Product2Id`, `Name`, and `UseStandardPrice` from the `Price Book Entry` object. The API name of the `Price Book Entry` object in Salesforce is `PricebookEntry`.

> `PricebookEntry` is another Salesforce standard object. We store the list price of the product under the `Pricebook2` object in the `Pricebookentry` object.

A sample query is given as follows:

```
SELECT ProductCode, Product2Id, Name, UseStandardPrice FROM
PricebookEntry
```

Refer to the following screenshot:

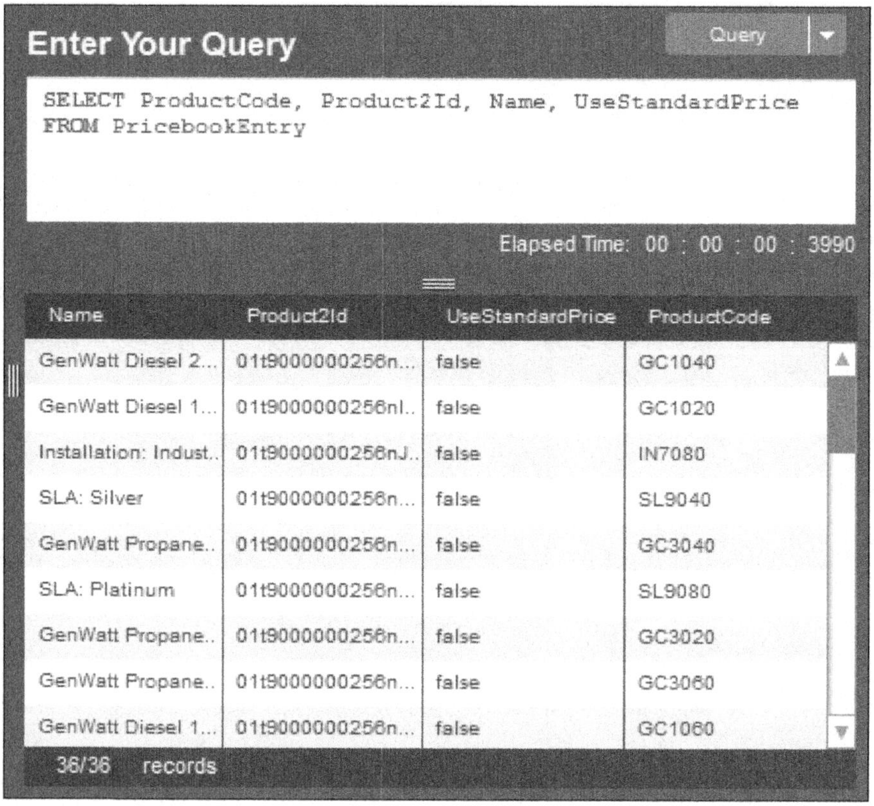

Summary

In this chapter, we learned what SOQL is and got to know its purpose. While discussing the purpose, we saw where exactly we use SOQL statements in Salesforce development and administration.

We discussed the fetching of the API name of the custom object with detailed descriptions and steps. Moreover, we saw the steps for fetching API names of the standard and the custom fields. The usage of system fields and querying system fields, with a description of each system field, was provided in a table.

Basic syntax of SOQL statements with all reserved keywords was discussed. We also saw some examples for fetching records using the SOQL queries from standard objects and custom objects. Finally, methods to find the difference between custom objects and standard objects and custom fields and standard fields were introduced.

2

Basic SOQL Statements

This chapter will teach us the usage of the alias notation, logical operators, comparison operators, the `IN` operator, the `NOT IN` operator, the `INCLUDES` operator, and the `EXCLUDES` operator while building SOQL queries. The different types of operators available are mainly used for filtering the records retrieved via the SOQL query.

The `WHERE` clause usage for filtering the records will also be explained. We will also learn how to sort the retrieved records while querying using the `ORDER BY` clause. By using the `ORDER BY` clause, we will be sorting our fetched records in both ascending and descending order.

The alias notation

SOQL supports the alias notation. The alias notation in SOQL is usually used to distinguish different objects used in a single SOQL.

The name used for the alias notation is very important. The SOQL reserved keywords that cannot be used as alias names are `AND`, `ASC`, `DESC`, `EXCLUDES`, `FIRST`, `FROM`, `GROUP`, `HAVING`, `IN`, `INCLUDES`, `LAST`, `LIKE`, `LIMIT`, `NOT`, `NULL`, `NULLS`, `OR`, `SELECT`, `WHERE`, and `WITH`. Naming should be done in a way that denotes the object, which will help us when we write some complex SOQL statements.

Let us see a simple example to understand the usage of the alias notation in SOQL.

A sample query is given as follows:

```
SELECT Acct.Id, Acct.Name FROM Account Acct
```

In the preceding example, `Acct` is the alias notation for the `Account` object. We can directly fetch `Id` and `Name` of the `Account` object without using the alias notation as well. This query is just for understanding the usage of the alias notation. Further examples will be concerned more with objects in querying. We will get a clear picture about the usage of the alias notation in this chapter. The following screenshot shows the output of the SOQL execution:

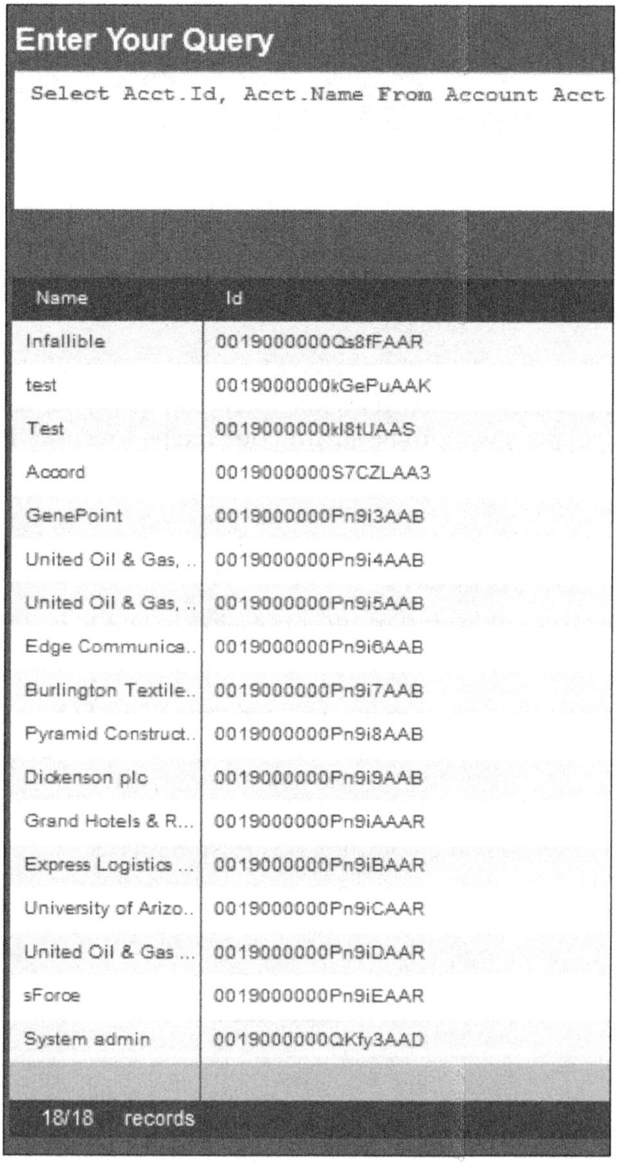

So far, we are aware of using the alias notation in SOQL statements in Salesforce.com. With the help of the preceding example, we have queried records using the SOQL query from only one object. Let's see some complex examples to understand how the alias notation in SOQL statements work to distinguish different objects used in SOQL statements.

A sample query is given as follows:

```
SELECT FirstName, LastName FROM Contact Con, Con.Account Acct WHERE Acct.
Name = 'Infallible'
```

In the preceding example, `Acct` is the alias notation for the `Account` object and `Con` is the alias notation for the `Contact` object. The alias notation will be very helpful to us while writing the SOQL queries for querying the records from multiple objects. Since many fields are common in all the objects, this alias notation helps us to distinguish among the objects used in the query. The following screenshot is the output of the SOQL execution:

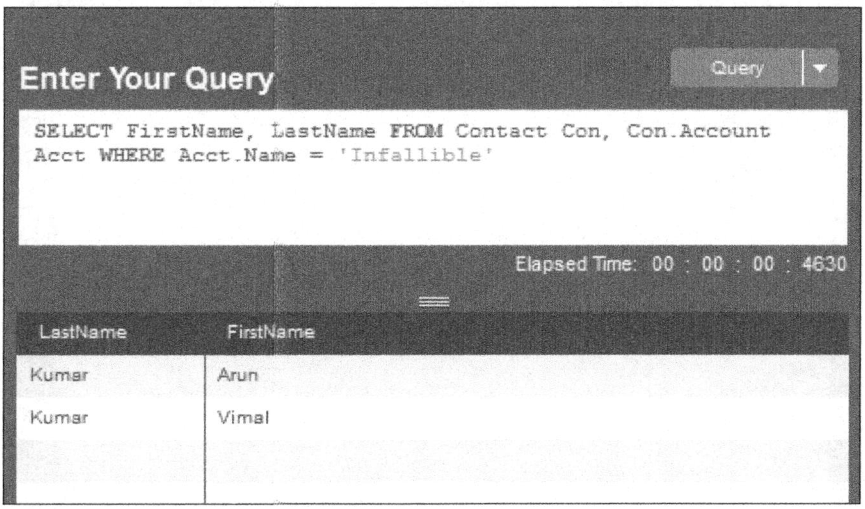

The WHERE clause

The `WHERE` clause in SOQL is mainly used to filter retrieved data. The `WHERE` clause in SOQL is also called the condition expression. Whenever we want to filter our records from the objects using SOQL, we have to make use of the `WHERE` clause. The `WHERE` clause will retrieve the records that match the criterion or criteria. Followed by the `WHERE` clause, we can use the comparison operators, logical operators, `IN` operator, `NOT IN` operator, `INCLUDES` operator, `EXCLUDES` operator, and so on. We have the privilege of using a combination of these operators to filter correctly in a SOQL statement.

Let us see an example showing the usage of the `WHERE` clause. A sample query is given as follows:

```
SELECT FirstName, LastName FROM Contact WHERE FirstName != null
```

In the preceding example, the SOQL query will return all the `Contact` records where `FirstName` of the contacts is not `null`. The following screenshot is the output of the SOQL execution:

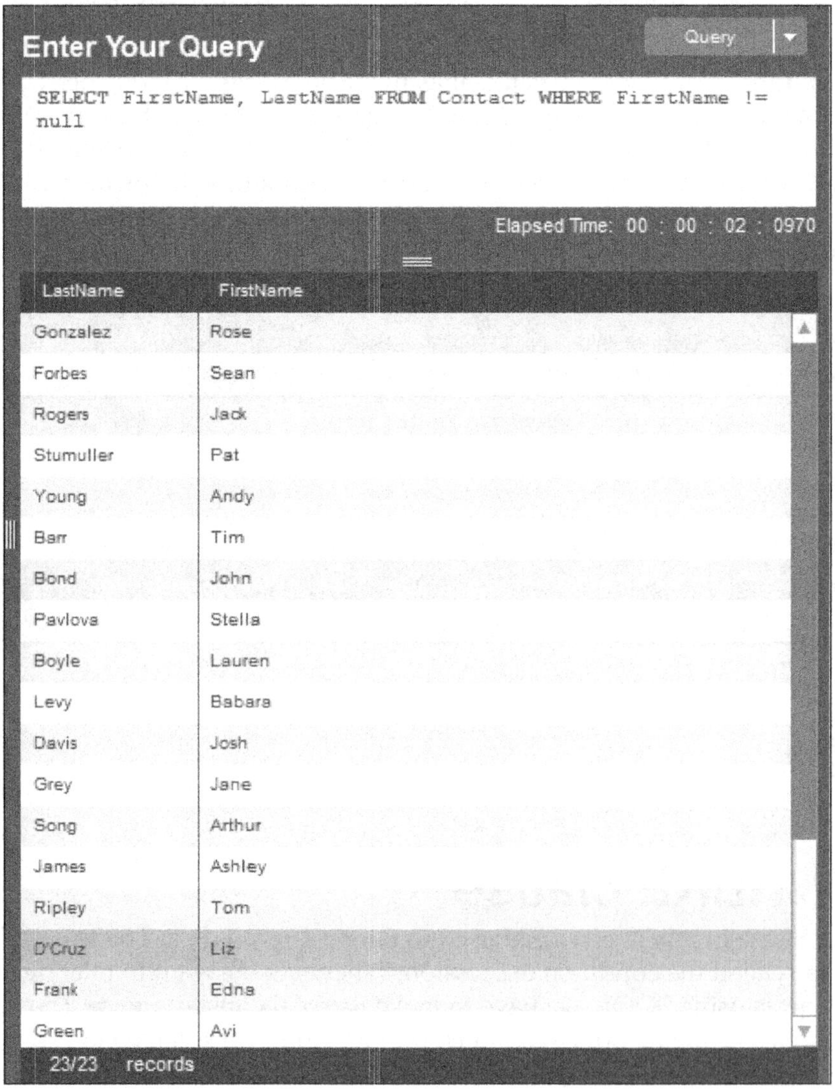

In the preceding example, we saw how to filter the `null` value records using the `WHERE` clause. In the same example, if we used the equals operator instead of the not equals operator, we would have retrieved records where the `FirstName` object of the contacts is null. With a small change, the query results differently. So, make sure to write your queries accurately. Let us see another example. A sample query is given as follows:

```
SELECT FirstName, LastName FROM Contact WHERE LastName = 'Bond'
```

In the preceding example, the SOQL query will return all the contacts where `LastName` is `Bond`. The preceding example with the condition `LastName = 'BOND'` will also produce the same result set since the SOQL string comparison is case insensitive. The following screenshot is the output of the SOQL execution:

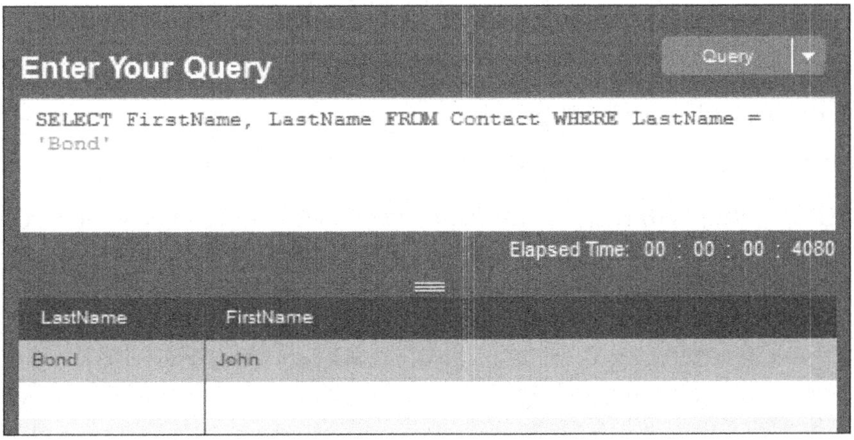

The comparison operators

Comparison operators are used in SOQL to compare a value with another value to return `true` or `false`. While using comparison operators, we should be very careful with data types. We should not compare number values with strings. We have to make sure we are comparing the values with proper data to avoid warnings and errors in SOQL.

Let us see the comparison operators that can be used in SOQL:

Operator	Description
`=`	Equals
`!=`	Not equals
`<`	Less than

Operator	Description
`<=`	Less than or equal to
`>`	Greater than
`>=`	Greater than or equal to
`LIKE`	Like

Let's see some examples of these comparison operators in SOQL.

The equals operator

Using the equals operator, we can retrieve records that match the given criteria. The equals operator checks whether the values of two operands are equal. If the value is equal, the condition becomes `true`. We can make use of the equals operator if we know which value we have to compare with.

A sample query is given as follows:

```
SELECT FirstName, LastName FROM Contact WHERE LastName = 'Bond'
```

The preceding query will retrieve all the contacts where the last name of the contact is `Bond`. The following screenshot is the output of the SOQL execution:

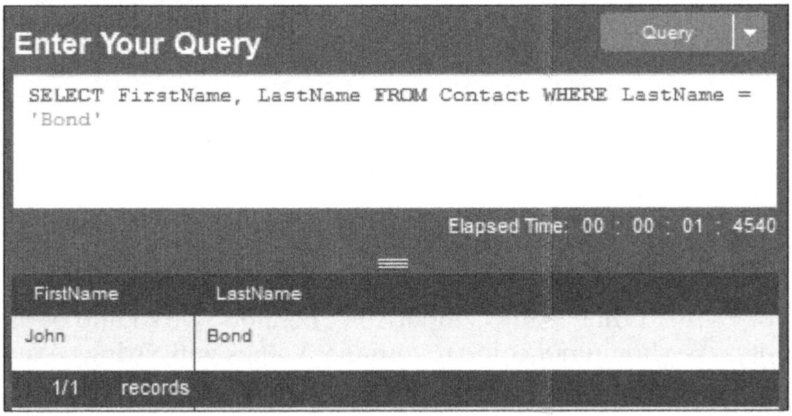

The not equals operator

Using the not equals operator, we can retrieve records that do not match the given criteria. The not equals operator checks whether the values of two operands are equal. If the value is not equal, the condition becomes `true`. We can make use of the not equals operator to retrieve accurate data if we know the exact value that should not be included.

A sample query is given as follows:

```
SELECT FirstName, LastName FROM Contact WHERE LastName != 'Bond'
```

The preceding query will retrieve all the contacts where the last name of the contacts is not `Bond`. The following screenshot is the output of the SOQL execution:

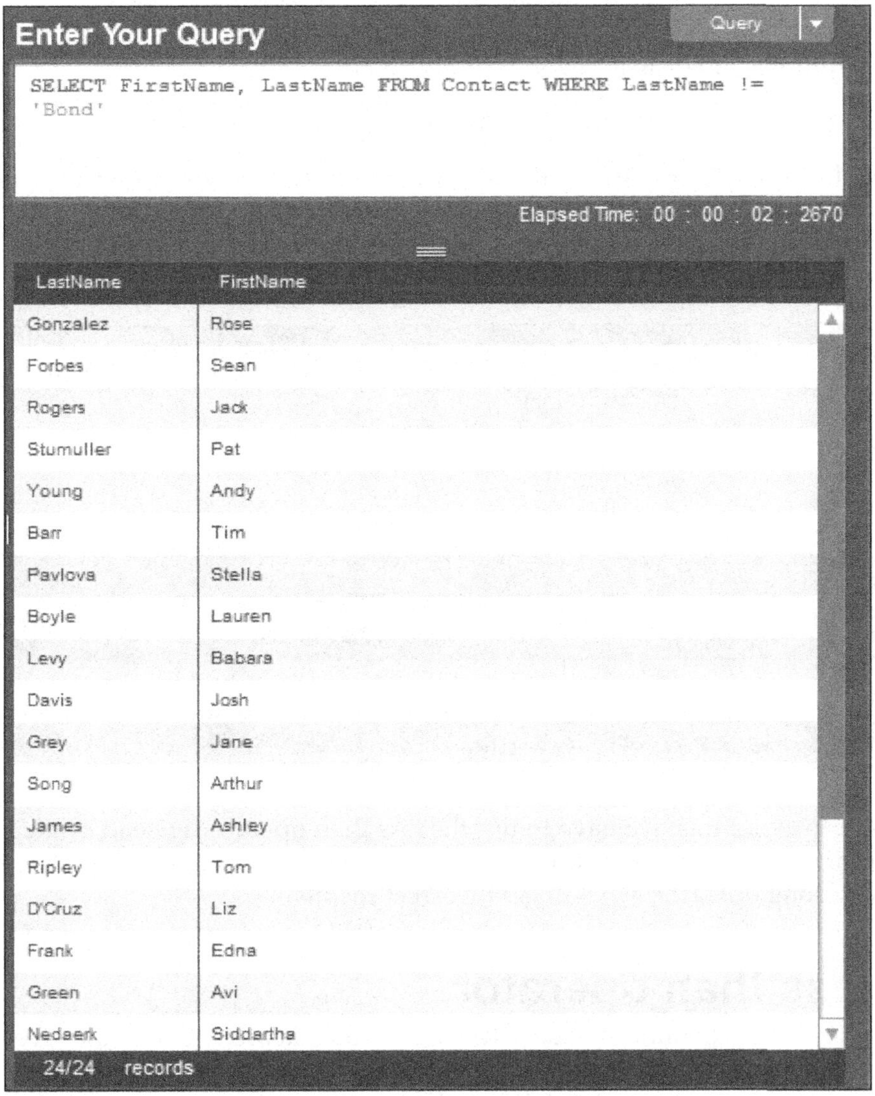

The less than or equal to operator

Using the less than or equal to operator, we can retrieve records that are less than or equal to the given limit. The less than or equal to operator is used to check whether the value of the left operand is less than or equal to the value of the right operand. If yes, the condition becomes `true`. The record that matches the given limit will also be included in the result.

A sample query is given as follows:

```
SELECT Name, Amount FROM Opportunity WHERE Amount <= 1000
```

The preceding query will retrieve all `Opportunity` instances where `Amount` is less than or equal to `1000`. If the `Amount` object is exactly equal to `1000`, those `Opportunity` instances are also included in the result. The following screenshot is the output of the SOQL execution:

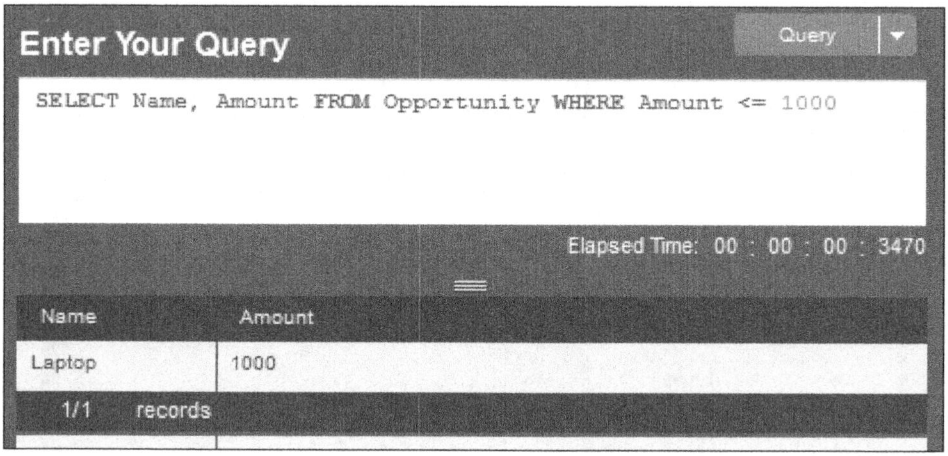

If we want to avoid this, we have to use the less than operator instead of the less than or equal to operator. We should be very careful when choosing the operator. If we select the wrong operator, we will get incorrect results.

The less than operator

Using the less than operator, we can retrieve records that are less than the given limit. The less than operator is used to check whether the value of the left operand is less than the value of the right operand. If yes, the condition becomes `true`. The less than operator does not include records that match the given limit, unlike the less than or equal to operator. In the less than operator, the limit is not included in the result. But in the case of the less than or equal to operator, the limit is included in the result.

A sample query is given as follows:

```
SELECT Name, Amount FROM Opportunity WHERE Amount < 10000
```

The preceding query will retrieve all `Opportunity` instances where `Amount` is less than `10000`. The following screenshot is the output of the SOQL execution:

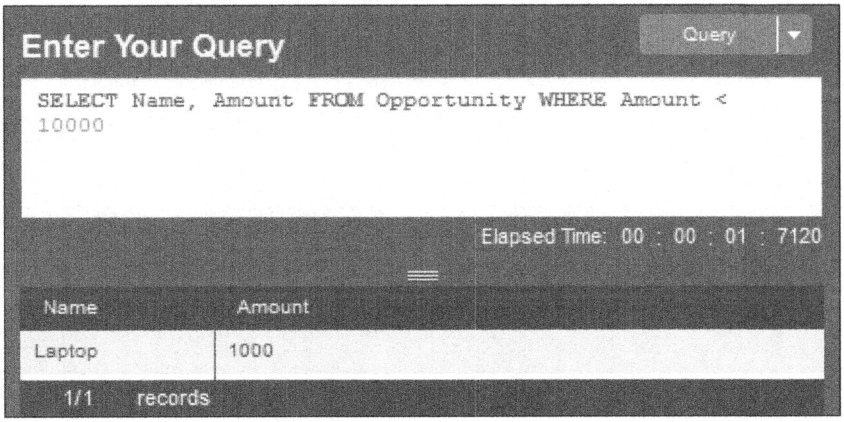

The `Opportunity` instances where `Amount` is exactly equal to `10000` are not included in the result. If we want to include this, we have to make use of the less than or equal to operator instead of the less than operator.

We need to ensure our symbol for the operator is correct, or else we will get incorrect results. If we are not careful, we may get the wrong set of data in our results. We have to check whether the symbol used is correct. A table with the list of operators and descriptions will help us a lot to avoid incorrect data while retrieving.

The greater than or equal to operator

Using the greater than or equal to operator, we can retrieve the records that are greater than or equal to the given limit. The greater than or equal to operator is used to check whether the value of the left operand is greater than or equal to the value of the right operand. If yes, the condition becomes `true`. The limit is also included in the result.

A sample query is given as follows:

```
SELECT Name, Amount FROM Opportunity WHERE Amount >= 1000
```

The preceding query will retrieve all the `Opportunity` instances where `Amount` is greater than or equal to `1000`. The `Opportunity` instances where the `Amount` object is exactly equal to `1000` are also included in the result. If we don't want to include those, we have to use the greater than operator instead. The choice of operator makes a big difference in the retrieved records count. The following screenshot is the output of the SOQL execution:

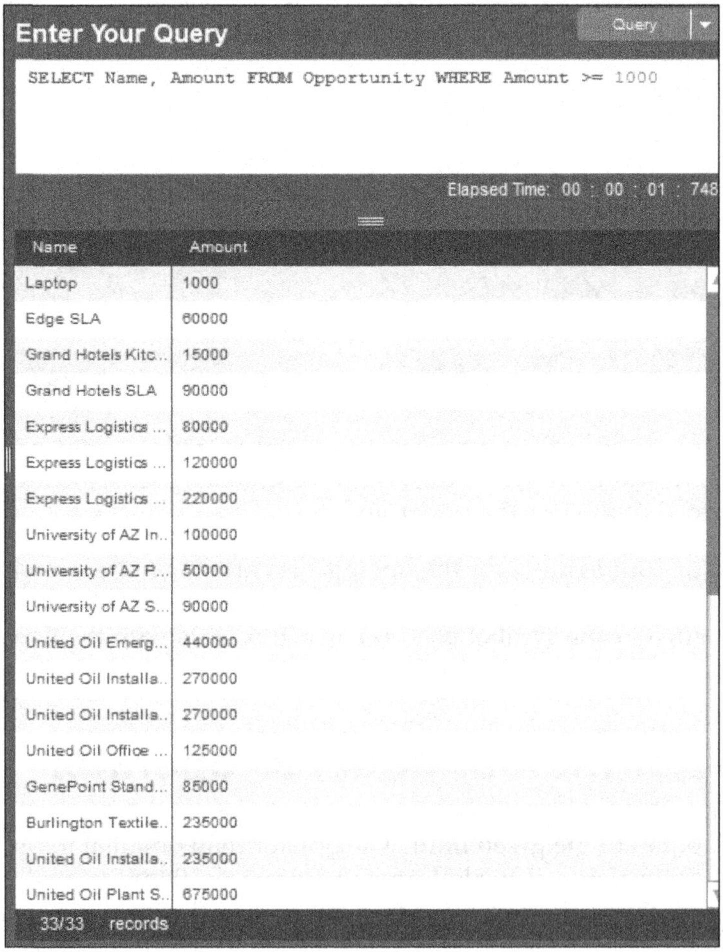

The greater than operator

Using the greater than operator, we can retrieve records that are greater than the given limit. The greater than operator is used to check whether the value of the left operand is greater than the value of the right operand. If yes, the condition becomes `true`.

A sample query is given as follows:

```
SELECT Name, Amount FROM Opportunity WHERE Amount > 1000
```

The preceding query will retrieve all the `Opportunity` instances where `Amount` is greater than `1000`. The following screenshot is the output of the SOQL execution:

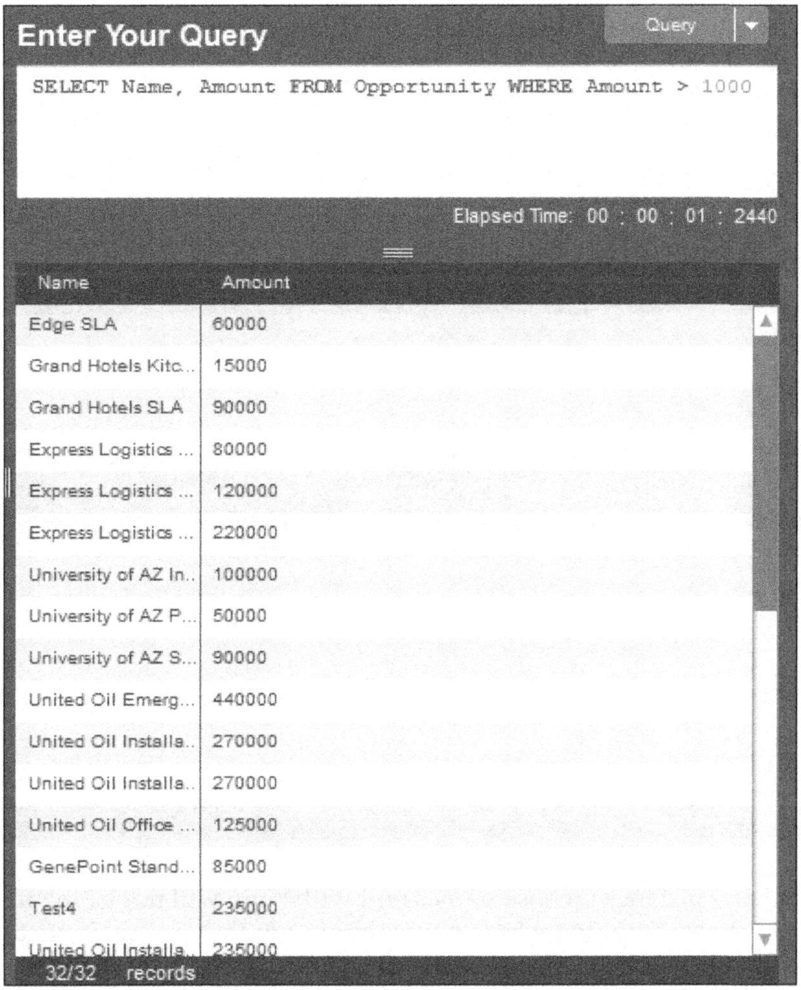

The `Opportunity` instances where the `Amount` object is exactly equal to `1000` are not included in the results. If we want to include `1000` in our results, we have to use the greater than or equal to operator instead.

The LIKE operator

Using the `LIKE` operator, we can retrieve records that match the substring provided. The `LIKE` operator is mainly used to compare a value to all similar values using wildcard characters. The `LIKE` operator is also called the pattern matching filtering technique. Any record that matches the pattern alone will be retrieved, which improves the filtering.

A sample query is given as follows:

```
SELECT Name, Amount FROM Opportunity WHERE Name LIKE 'Test%'
```

The preceding query will retrieve all the `Opportunity` instances where the name starts with `Test`. The following screenshot is the output of the SOQL execution:

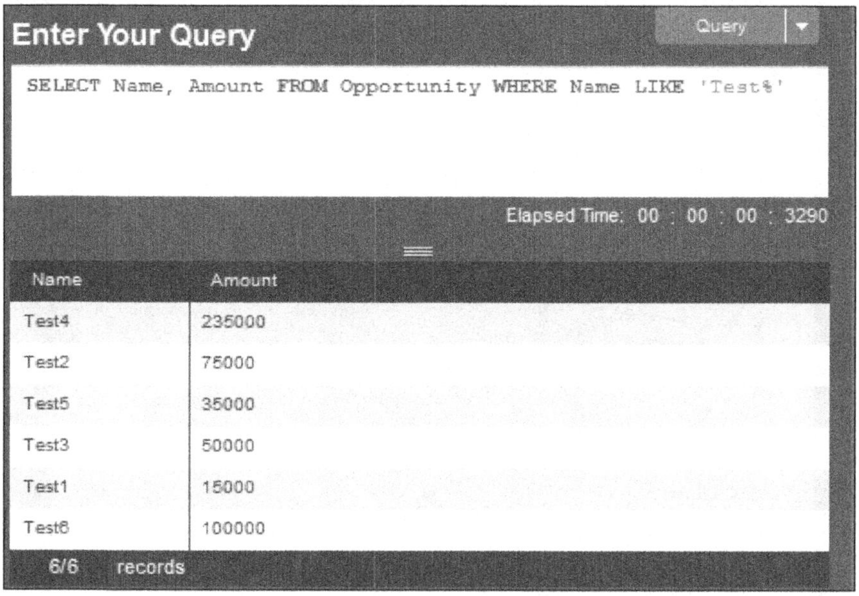

The `Opportunity` instances whose names end with `Test` will not be included in the results. If we also want to include names ending with `Test`, we have to use another percentage symbol to the left so that it will be `'%Test%'`. When we do this, any `Opportunity` instance with `Name` that includes `Test` will also be included in the result. We have to use _ instead of `%` if we want to just match it with a single character to its left or right. The `LIKE` operator is very useful if we are unsure about the exact value with which we have to match. While using the `LIKE` operator, make sure you have entered the correct matching pattern. For example, the `'%Test%'` matching pattern will not be as efficient as `'Test%'` due to the way indexes work and may take a longer time to retrieve the result set of a large object.

The IN operator

The `IN` operator is used to specify multiple values in the `WHERE` clause for matching and filtering records. The SOQL query will fetch records that match the values specified. The `IN` operator is mainly used to compare a value to a list of values that have been specified, and it retrieves the records if it matches the values specified in the list. The `IN` operator is used if you want to compare a value with multiple values to ensure the retrieved records are accurate.

A sample query is given as follows:

```
SELECT FirstName, LastName FROM Contact WHERE FirstName IN ('Rose',
'Sean', 'Jack', 'Test')
```

The preceding query will return all contacts where the first name matches the values specified. Here, the values inside the brackets are case insensitive for the `IN` operator. The following screenshot is the output of the SOQL execution:

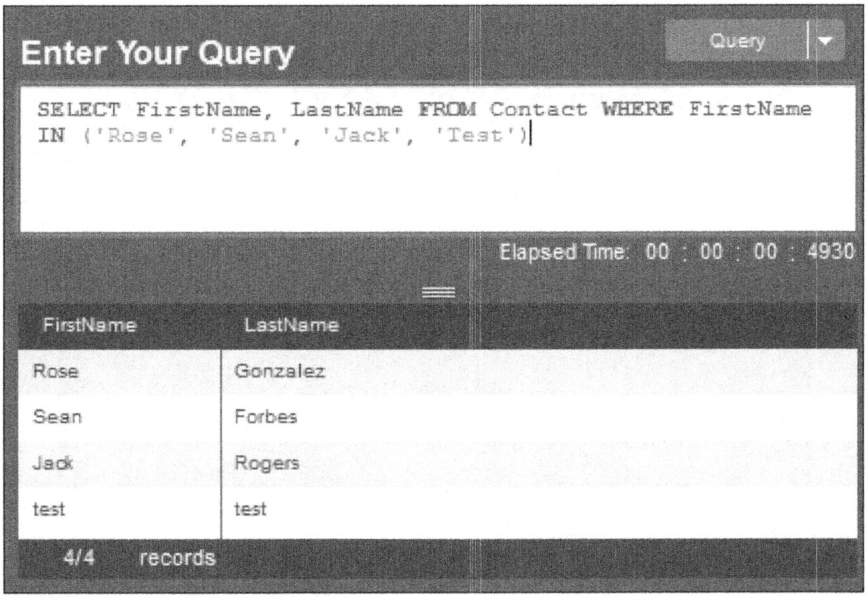

The NOT IN operator

The `NOT IN` operator is used to specify multiple values in the `WHERE` clause for unmatching and filtering records. The SOQL will fetch records that do not match the values specified. The `NOT IN` operator is mainly used to compare a value to a list of values that have been specified, and it retrieves the records if it does not match the values specified in the list.

The `NOT IN` operator works in an opposite manner to the `IN` operator. It retrieves records that do not match the values specified, whereas the `IN` operator retrieves records that match the values specified.

A sample query is given as follows:

```
SELECT FirstName, LastName FROM Contact WHERE FirstName NOT IN ('Rose',
'Sean', 'Jack', 'Test')
```

The preceding query will return all the contacts where the first name does not match the values specified. The following screenshot is the output of the SOQL execution:

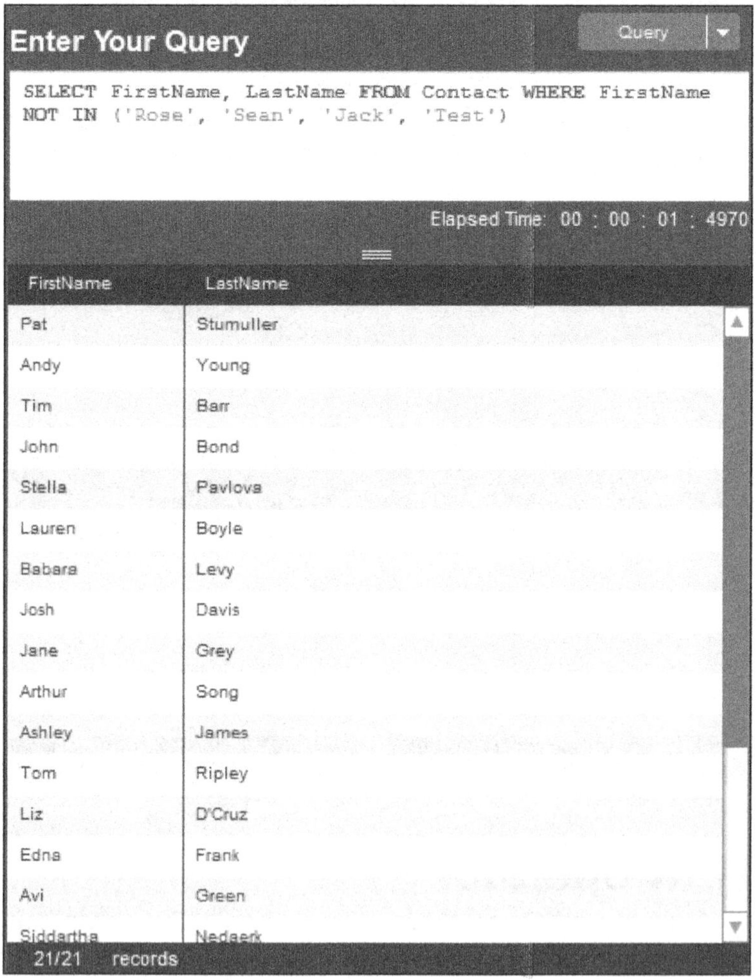

The result does not contain records that match the specified values.

The logical operators

The concept behind logical operators is simple and easy. Logical operators are mainly used to check multiple conditions in a single SOQL statement. Logical operators are connectors for connecting one or more conditions inside a single SOQL statement. It combines the conditions so that we can filter our records to be retrieved very accurately. Logical operator will return either `true` or `false`.

The two logical operators available in SOQL are the following:

- `AND`
- `OR`

The AND operator

Using the `AND` operator, we can retrieve records that satisfy all the conditions specified. If a record matches the first condition and does not match the second condition, the record will not be retrieved. For example, say the condition states that the `city` parameter should be equal to `Chennai` and the `postal code` parameter should not be null; if a record's `city` parameter is `Chennai` and `postal code` is null, the record will not be retrieved.

The OR operator

Using the `OR` operator, we can retrieve records that satisfy any one of the conditions specified. If a record matches the first condition and does not match the second condition, the record will be retrieved and vice versa. For example, say the condition states that the `city` parameter should be equal to `Chennai` or `Bangalore` and if a record's `city` parameter is `Mysore` for a record, the record will not be retrieved. However, if the `city` parameter is `Chennai` for a record, that record will be included in the results.

The use of `AND` and `OR` together is allowed in SOQL to filter our records to avoid unwanted ones in our result. The use of `AND` and `OR` together helps us in many ways to fetch our required records for manipulation.

A sample query for the `AND` operator is as follows:

```
SELECT Name, Amount FROM Opportunity WHERE Amount > 1000 AND Amount <
100000
```

The preceding query will retrieve opportunities where `Amount` is greater than `1000` and less than `100000`. The following screenshot is the output of the SOQL execution:

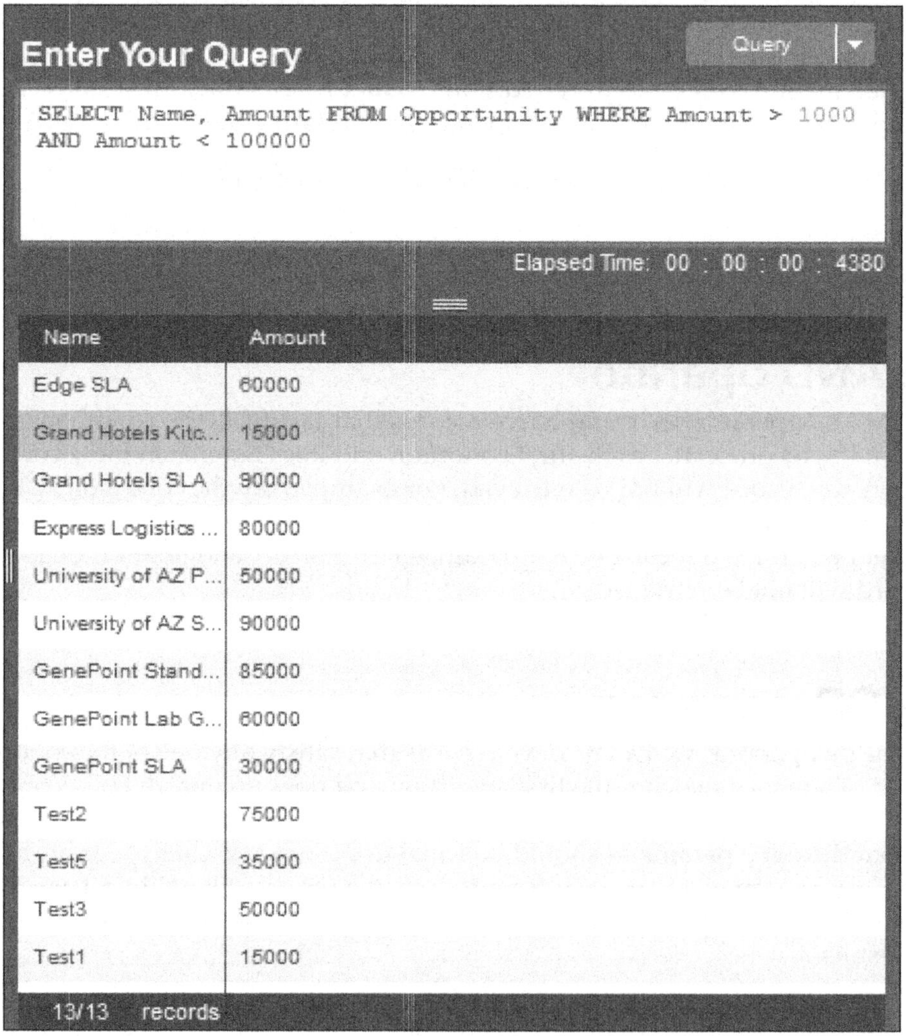

The `Opportunity` instances where amount is `1000` are not included in the result. If we want to include this, we have to use the greater than or equal to operator instead of the greater than operator.

A sample query for the `OR` operator is given as follows:

```
SELECT Name, Amount FROM Opportunity WHERE Name = 'Infallible' OR Name =
'Infallible Techie'
```

The preceding query will retrieve all the `Opportunity` instances where `Name` is `Infallible` or `Infallible Techie`. The following screenshot is the output of the SOQL execution:

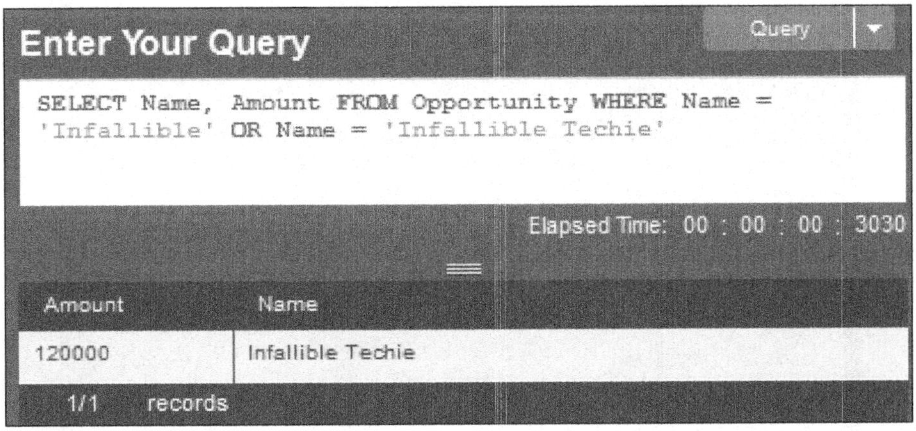

The ORDER BY clause

The `ORDER BY` clause in SOQL is used to sort the records retrieved in the ascending or descending order.

An ascending order sample query is given as follows:

```
SELECT Name, Amount FROM Opportunity ORDER BY Name ASC
```

The preceding query will retrieve all the `Opportunity` instances arranged in the ascending order of the name. The following screenshot is the output of the SOQL execution:

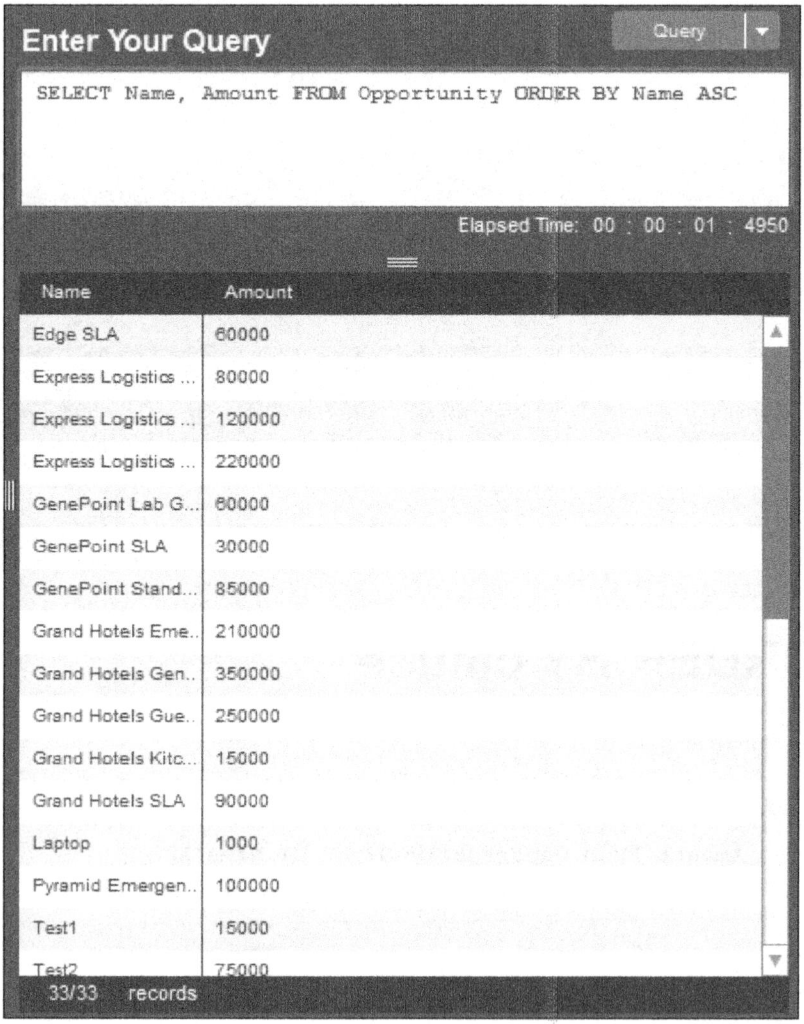

A descending order sample query is given as follows:

```
SELECT Name, Amount FROM Opportunity ORDER BY Name DESC
```

The preceding query will retrieve all the `Opportunity` instances arranged in the descending order of the name. The following screenshot is the output of the SOQL execution:

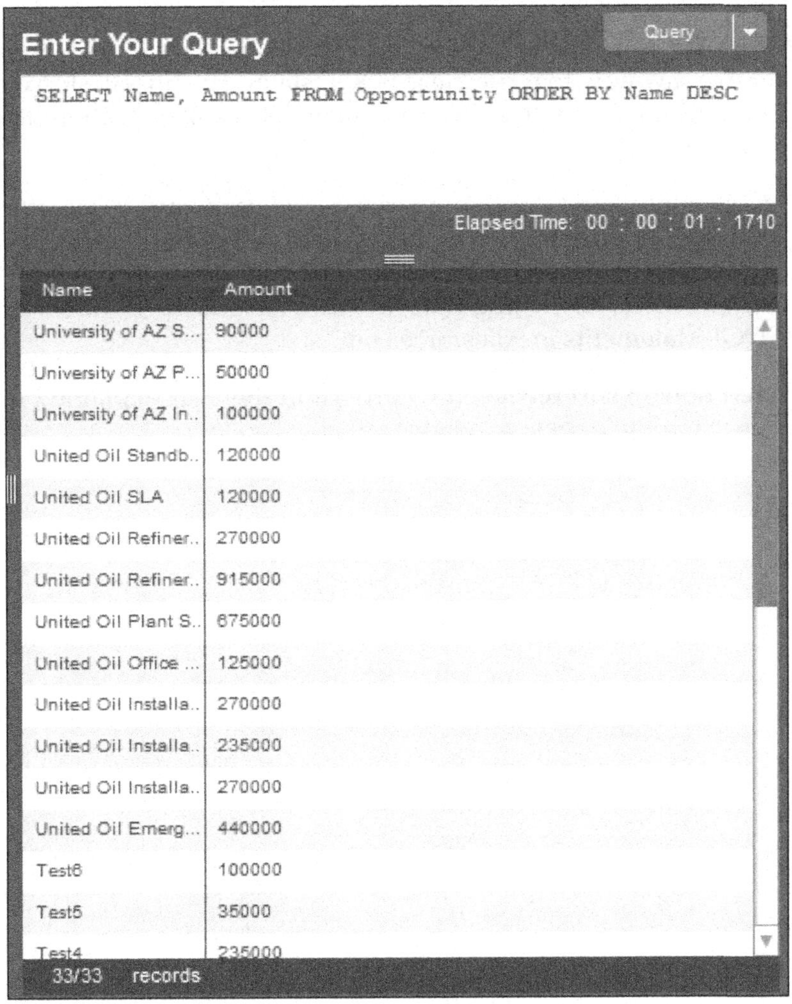

Here, ASC means ascending order and DESC means descending order. By default, it will always be ascending order.

The INCLUDES and EXCLUDES operators

The `INCLUDES` and `EXCLUDES` operators are mainly used for filtering the multipick `list` field in Salesforce.com. The standard way to filter multipick `list` field values in SOQL is using the `INCLUDES` and `EXCLUDES` operators. These operators are discussed in detail in *Chapter 3, Advanced SOQL Statements with Examples*.

Summary

In this chapter, we saw how to write basic SOQL statements in Salesforce.com. We started with a simple alias notation. We tried many examples to differentiate objects using alias notation.

Later, we saw the logical operators, comparison operators, the `IN` operator, and the `NOT IN` operator. The logical operators `AND` and `OR` were explained in detail. The comparison operators, `=`, `!=`, `<`, `>`, `<=`, `>=`, and `LIKE`, were also explained in detail. We learned where, when, and the ways in which these operators can be used in our SOQL statements in Salesforce.com.

We also covered how to sort retrieved records, and this was explained with sample queries using the `ORDER BY` clause.

3

Advanced SOQL Statements

In the previous chapter, we saw the basic SOQL statements that deal with one object in a SOQL statement. This chapter gives more information on how to write advanced SOQL statements. This chapter deals with querying the records for one or more objects in a single SOQL statement. In this case, there should be some relationship among the objects. In Salesforce.com, we cannot query the records from two or more objects if they don't have a relationship between them. The relationships that are available in Salesforce.com are **lookup** relationship and **master-detail** relationship.

Filtering a multiselect picklist field using the `INCLUDES` and `EXCLUDES` operators will be discussed in detail. In *Chapter 2, Basic SOQL Statements*, only the definition was given for the `INCLUDES` and `EXCLUDES` operators.

The grouping of records with more than one field using `GROUP BY ROLLUP` and `GROUP BY CUBE` will be explained here with examples. Sorting the records in both the ascending and descending orders together in a SOQL statement will also be further discussed.

Relationship queries

Relationship queries are mainly used to query the records from one or more objects in a single SOQL statement in Salesforce.com. As discussed earlier, we cannot query the records from more than one object without having a relationship between the objects.

Let us see an example for relationship queries with standard objects to query the records. The relationship between `Account` and `Contact` is a lookup. `Account` is the parent object, and `Contact` is the child object. `Account` can have multiple `Contacts`.

A sample query is given as follows:

```
SELECT Id, Name, (SELECT Id, Name FROM Contacts) FROM Account
```

The preceding query will retrieve all the accounts and their associated `Contacts`. The following screenshot shows the output of the SOQL execution:

Let us see another example for relationship queries with custom objects to query the records. The relationship between `Employee` and `Hobby` is a master-detail relationship. `Employee` is the parent object, and `Hobby` is the child object. `Employee` can have multiple `Hobbies`.

A sample query is given as follows:

```
SELECT Employee_Name__c, (SELECT Id, Name FROM Hobbies__r) FROM
Employee__c
```

The preceding query will retrieve all the names of the employees and their associated `Hobbies`. The following screenshot shows the output of the SOQL execution:

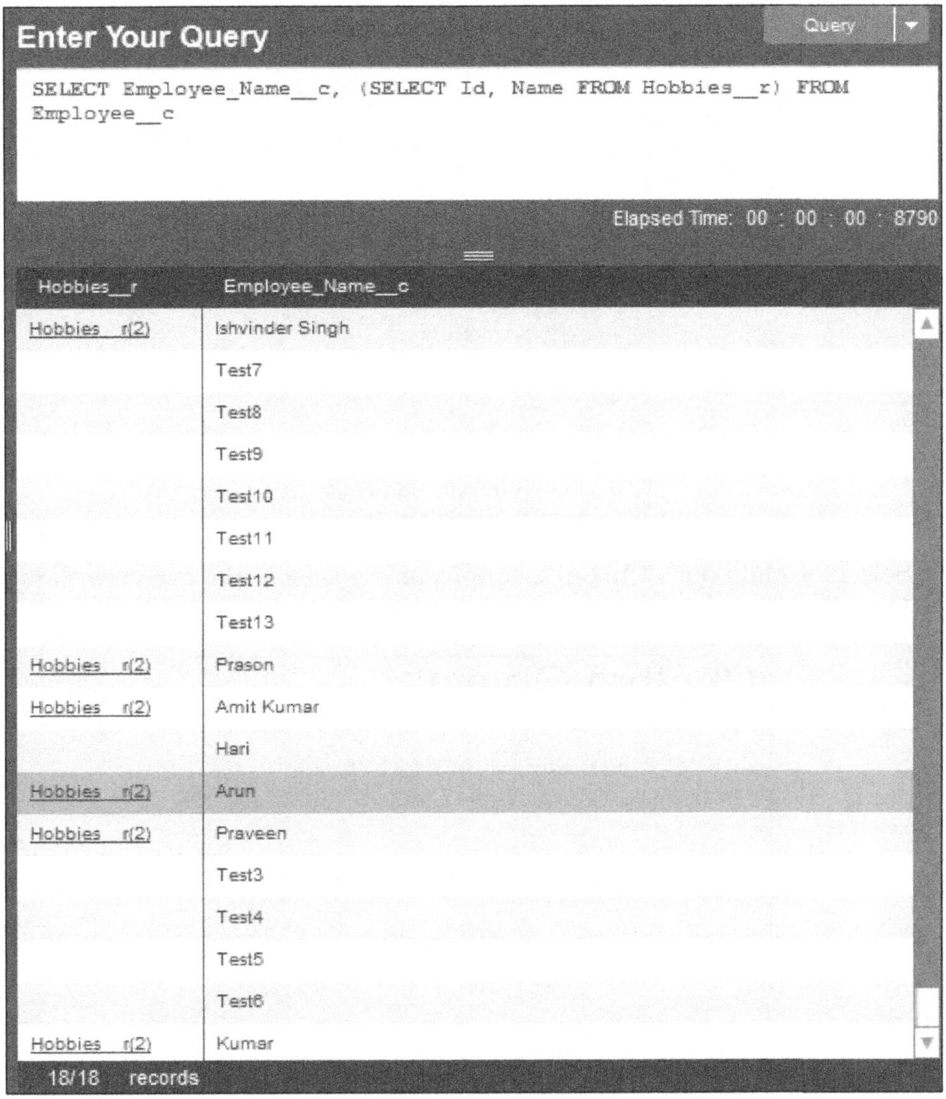

To find out the name of the relationship, go to the objects' definition and select the relationship field. The **Child Relationship Name** option gives us the relationship name. The `__r` symbol should be added along with the child relationship name to query in the case of custom relationships. For standard relationships, we should not add `__r`. The following steps will help us to get the relationship name for relationship queries:

1. Navigate to **Setup** | **Build** | **Create** | **Objects** as shown in the following screenshot:

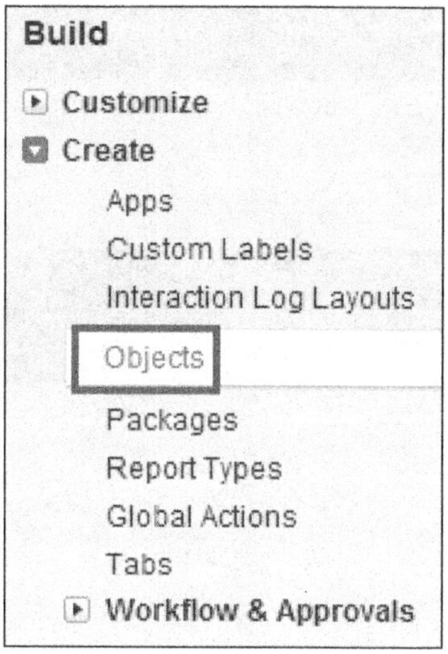

2. Select the child object. In our example, `Hobby` is our child object as shown in the following screenshot:

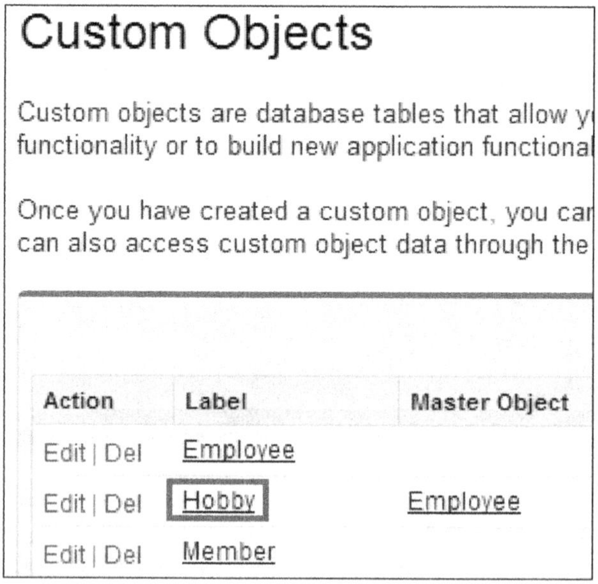

3. Select the relationship field:

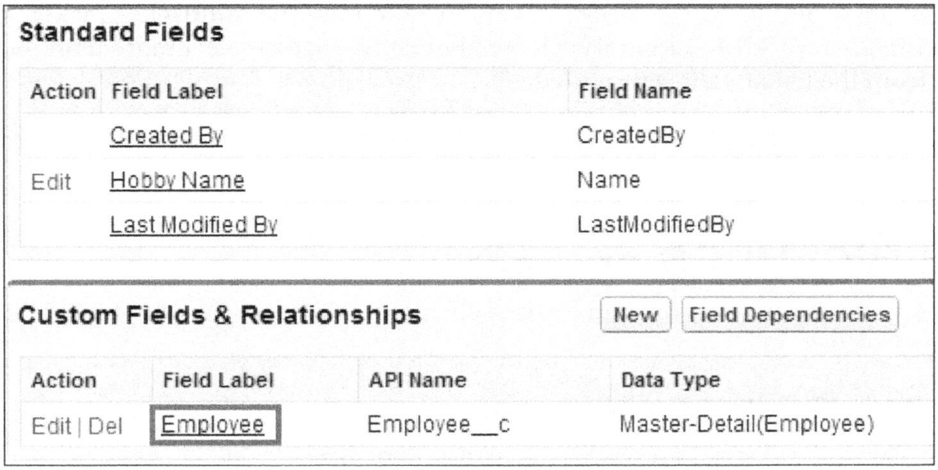

4. The **Child Relationship Name** option denotes the relationship name. We have to add `__r` to the child relationship name when querying the records using SOQL. In the case of a standard relationship, we need not add `__r` when we query the records using SOQL.

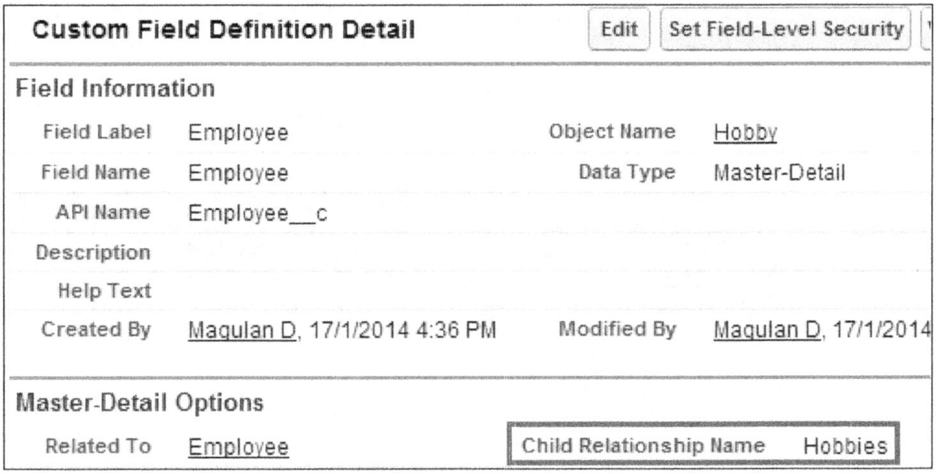

> A custom relationship in Salesforce.com always ends with `__r`. But a standard relationship, which exists between the standard Salesforce.com objects, does not end with `__r`.

Filtering multiselect picklist values

The `INCLUDES` and `EXCLUDES` operators are used to filter the multiselect picklist field. The multiselect picklist field in Salesforce allows the user to select more than one value from the list of values provided.

Let us see a few examples of filtering the multiselect picklist values. `Skills__c` is a multiselect picklist field.

The INCLUDES operator

The `INCLUDES` operator is used to retrieve the records that contain any one of the specified values.

A sample query is given as follows:

```
SELECT Employee_Name__c, Skills__c FROM Employee__c WHERE Skills__c
INCLUDES ('C', 'C#')
```

The preceding query will fetch the names of all the employees whose `Skills` match either with `C` or `C#`. The following screenshot is the output of the SOQL execution:

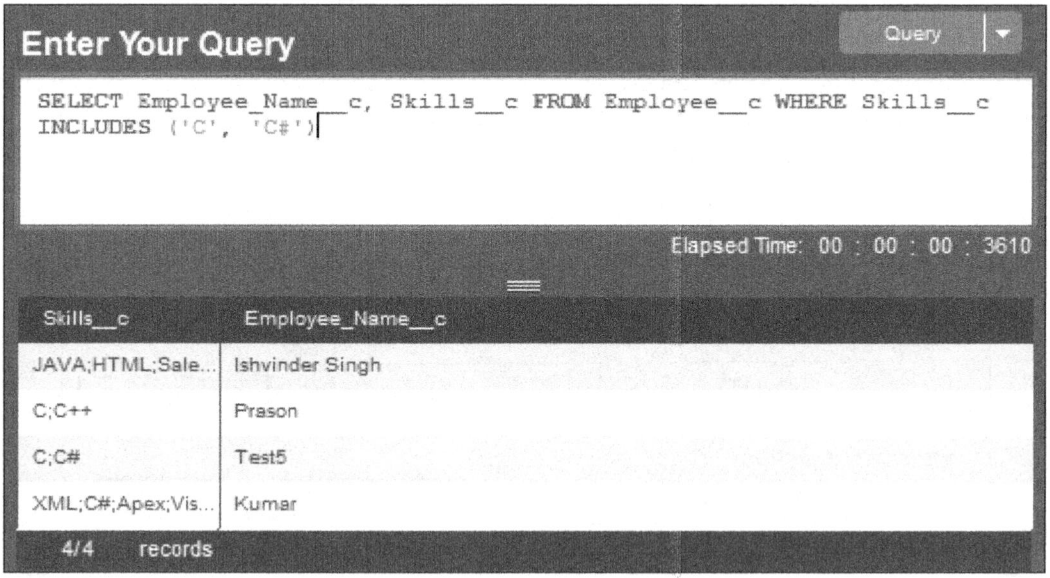

Let us see an example for including a null value.

A sample query is given as follows:

```
SELECT Employee_Name__c, Skills__c FROM Employee__c WHERE Skills__c
EXCLUDES ('C', 'C#', '')
```

The preceding query will fetch the names of all employees whose `Skills` match either with `C` or `C#` and null. The following screenshot shows the output of the SOQL execution:

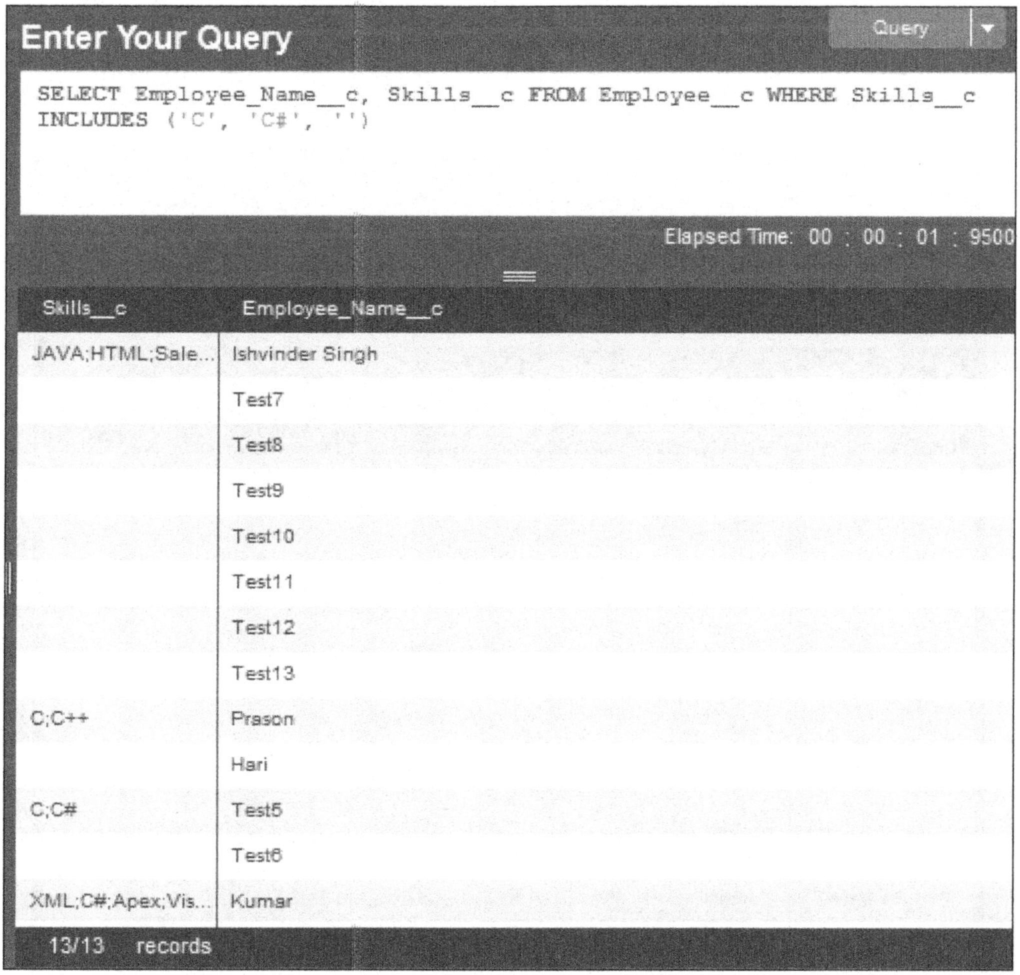

The EXCLUDES operator

The `EXCLUDES` operator is used to retrieve the records that do not contain any one of the specified values.

A sample query is given as follows:

```
SELECT Employee_Name__c, Skills__c FROM Employee__c WHERE Skills__c
EXCLUDES ('C', 'C#')
```

The preceding query will fetch the names of all employees whose `Skills` do not match either with `C` or `C#`. The following screenshot shows the output of the SOQL execution:

Let us see an example for excluding the null value.

A sample query is given as follows:

```
SELECT Employee_Name__c, Skills__c FROM Employee__c WHERE Skills__c
EXCLUDES ('C', 'C#', '')
```

The preceding query will fetch the names of all the employees whose `Skills` do not match either with `C` or `C#` and null. The following screenshot shows the output of the SOQL execution:

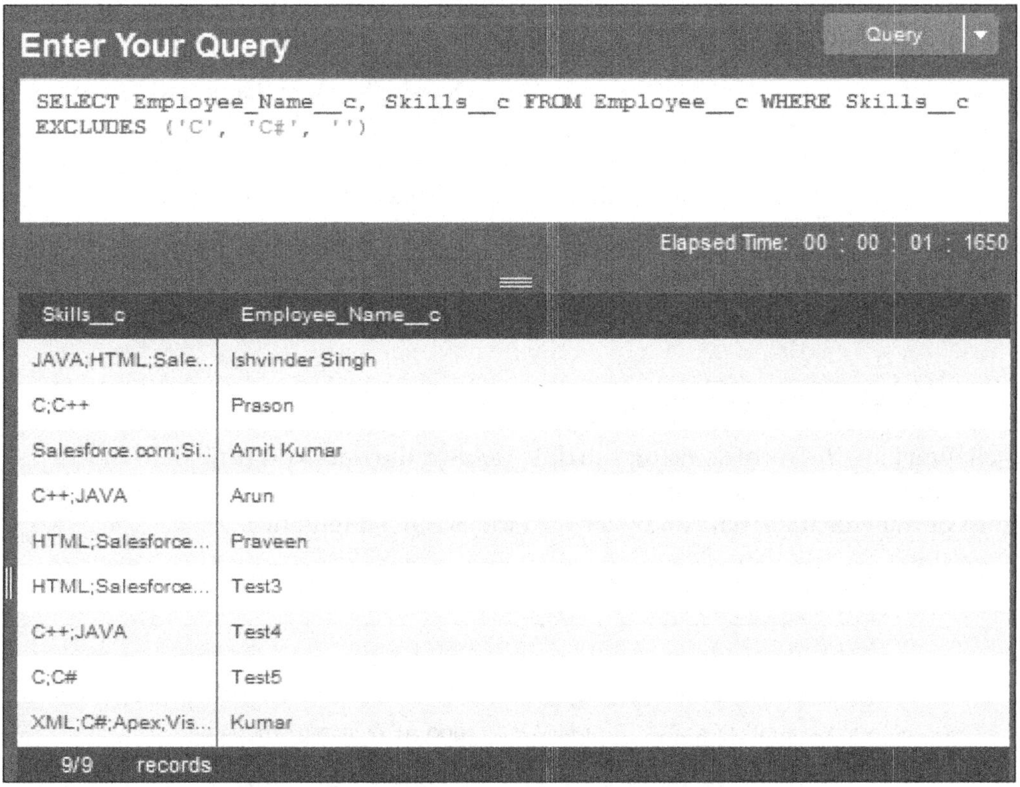

The escape sequences

An escape character is a character that invokes an alternative interpretation of the subsequent characters in a character sequence. The following table shows the list of escape sequences that can be used in the SOQL statements:

Sequence name	Description
`\n` or `\N`	New line
`\r` or `\R`	Carriage return
`\t` or `\T`	Tab
`\f` or `\F`	Form feed
`\b` or `\B`	Bell
`\"`	One double-quote character
`\'`	One single-quote character
`\\`	Backslash
The `LIKE` operator expression: `\_`	Matches a single underscore character (_)
The `LIKE` operator expression: `\%`	Matches a single percentage sign character (`%`)

The date formats

When querying the records using the date field or the date and time field in the SOQL statement, the date formats should be followed. The following table shows the list of date formats that can be used in the SOQL statements:

Format	Examples
YYYY-MM-DD	1999-01-01
YYYY-MM-DDThh:mm:ss+hh:mm	1999-01-01T23:01:01+01:00
YYYY-MM-DDThh:mm:ss-hh:mm	1999-01-01T23:01:01-08:00
YYYY-MM-DDThh:mm:ssZ	1999-01-01T23:01:01Z

The date literals

When querying the records using the date field in the SOQL statement, the date literals can be used. The following table shows the list of date literals that can be used in the SOQL statements:

Date literal	Sample query
YESTERDAY	SELECT Id FROM Employee__c WHERE Joining_Date__c = YESTERDAY
TODAY	SELECT Id FROM Employee__c WHERE Joining_Date__c > TODAY
TOMORROW	SELECT Id FROM Employee__c WHERE Joining Date__c = TOMORROW
LAST_WEEK	SELECT Id FROM Employee__c WHERE Joining_Date__c > LAST_WEEK
THIS_WEEK	SELECT Id FROM Employee__c WHERE Joining_Date__c < THIS_WEEK
NEXT_WEEK	SELECT Id FROM Employee__c WHERE Joining_Date__c = NEXT_WEEK
LAST_MONTH	SELECT Id FROM Employee__c WHERE Joining_Date__c > LAST_MONTH
THIS_MONTH	SELECT Id FROM Employee__c WHERE Joining_Date__c < THIS_MONTH
NEXT_MONTH	SELECT Id FROM Employee__c WHERE Joining_Date__c = NEXT_MONTH
LAST_90_DAYS	SELECT Id FROM Employee__c WHERE Joining_Date__c = LAST_90_DAYS
NEXT_90_DAYS	SELECT Id FROM Employee__c WHERE Joining_Date__c > NEXT_90_DAYS
LAST_N_DAYS:n	SELECT Id FROM Employee__c WHERE Joining_Date__c = LAST_N_DAYS:365
NEXT_N_DAYS:n	SELECT Id FROM Employee__c WHERE Joining_Date__c > NEXT_N_DAYS:15
THIS_QUARTER	SELECT Id FROM Employee__c WHERE Joining_Date__c = THIS_QUARTER
LAST_QUARTER	SELECT Id FROM Employee__c WHERE Joining_Date__c > LAST_QUARTER
NEXT_QUARTER	SELECT Id FROM Employee__c WHERE Joining_Date__c < NEXT_QUARTER

Date literal	Sample query
NEXT_N_QUARTERS:n	SELECT Id FROM Employee__c WHERE Joining_Date__c < NEXT_N_QUARTERS:2
LAST_N_QUARTERS:n	SELECT Id FROM Employee__c WHERE Joining_Date__c > LAST_N_QUARTERS:2
THIS_YEAR	SELECT Id FROM Employee__c WHERE Joining_Date__c = THIS_YEAR
LAST_YEAR	SELECT Id FROM Employee__c WHERE Joining_Date__c > LAST_YEAR
NEXT_YEAR	SELECT Id FROM Employee__c WHERE Joining_Date__c < NEXT_YEAR
NEXT_N_YEARS:n	SELECT Id FROM Employee__c WHERE Joining_Date__c < NEXT_N_YEARS:5
LAST_N_YEARS:n	SELECT Id FROM Employee__c WHERE Joining_Date__c > LAST_N_YEARS:5
THIS_FISCAL_QUARTER	SELECT Id FROM Employee__c WHERE Joining_Date__c = THIS_FISCAL_QUARTER
LAST_FISCAL_QUARTER	SELECT Id FROM Employee__c WHERE Joining_Date__c > LAST_FISCAL_QUARTER
NEXT_FISCAL_QUARTER	SELECT Id FROM Employee__c WHERE Joining_Date__c < NEXT_FISCAL_QUARTER
NEXT_N_FISCAL_QUARTERS:n	SELECT Id FROM Employee__c WHERE Joining_Date__c < NEXT_N_FISCAL_QUARTERS:6
LAST_N_FISCAL_QUARTERS:n	SELECT Id FROM Employee__c WHERE Joining_Date__c > LAST_N_FISCAL_QUARTERS:6
THIS_FISCAL_YEAR	SELECT Id FROM Employee__c WHERE Joining_Date__c = THIS_FISCAL_YEAR

Date literal	Sample query
`LAST_FISCAL_YEAR`	`SELECT Id FROM Employee__c WHERE Joining_Date__c > LAST_FISCAL_YEAR`
`NEXT_FISCAL_YEAR`	`SELECT Id FROM Employee__c WHERE Joining_Date__c < NEXT_FISCAL_YEAR`
`NEXT_N_FISCAL_YEARS:n`	`SELECT Id FROM Employee__c WHERE Joining_Date__c < NEXT_N_FISCAL_YEARS:3`
`LAST_N_FISCAL_YEARS:n`	`SELECT Id FROM Employee__c WHERE Joining_Date__c > LAST_N_FISCAL_YEARS:3`

Querying with the date fields

Let us see an example for querying with the date field using one of the date literals we just covered.

A sample query is given as follows:

```
SELECT Employee_Name__c, Joining_Date__c FROM Employee__c WHERE Joining_
Date__c < LAST_MONTH
```

The preceding query will fetch the names of all the employees whose joining date values are less than the values for the current date last month. The following screenshot shows the output of the SOQL execution:

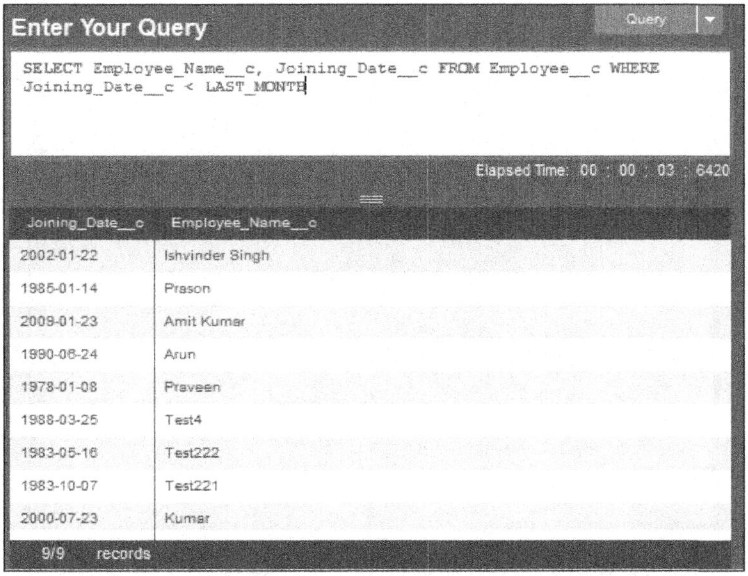

Sorting in both the ascending and descending orders

Sometimes, we may get a chance to sort the records when we fetch these using the SOQL statements based on two fields, one field in the ascending order and another field in the descending order. The following sample query will help us to achieve this easily:

```
SELECT Name, Industry FROM Account ORDER By Name ASC, Industry DESC
```

Using the preceding SOQL query, the accounts will first be sorted by `Name` in the ascending order and then by `Industry` in the descending order. The following screenshot shows the output of the SOQL execution:

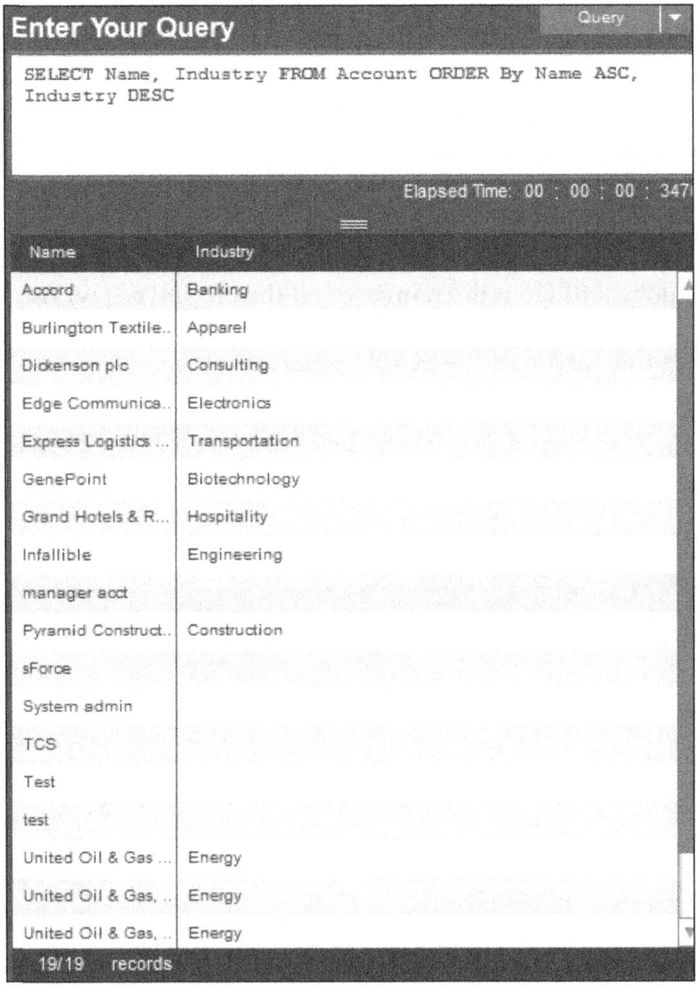

First, the records are arranged in the ascending order of the account's `Name`, and then it is sorted by `Industry` in the descending order.

Using the GROUP BY ROLLUP clause

The `GROUP BY ROLLUP` clause is used to add subtotals for aggregated data in query results. A query with a `GROUP BY ROLLUP` clause returns the same aggregated data as an equivalent query with a `GROUP BY` clause. It also returns multiple levels of subtotal rows. You can include up to three fields in a comma-separated list in a `GROUP BY ROLLUP` clause.

A sample query is given as follows:

```
SELECT City__c, State__c, COUNT(Employee_Name__c) Counts FROM Employee__c
GROUP BY ROLLUP(City__c, State__c)
```

The following screenshot shows the output of the SOQL execution:

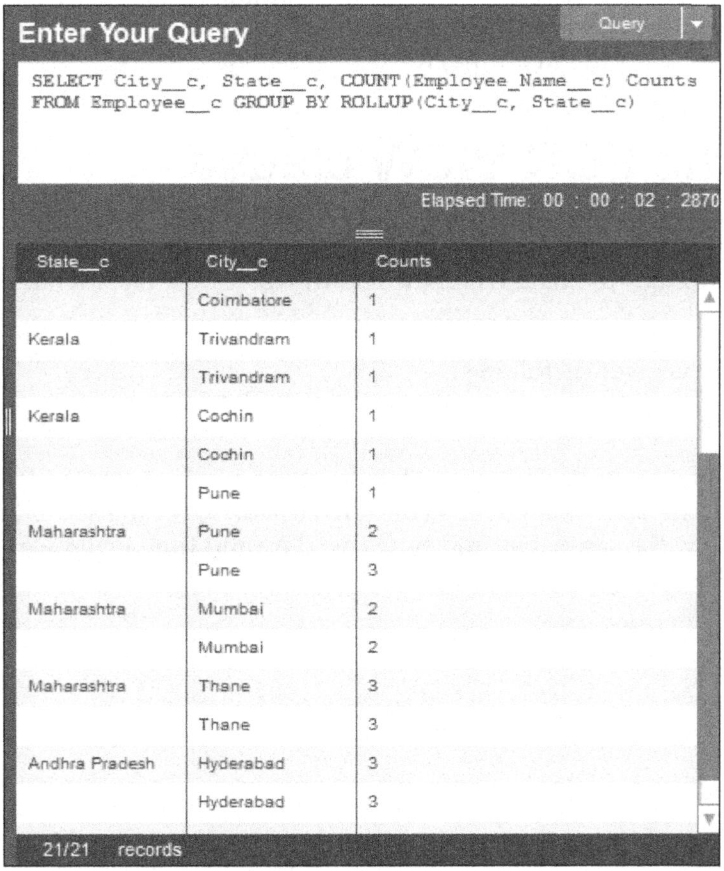

In the previous example, we saw both the statewise and citywise count. This `GROUP BY ROLLUP` clause will be very useful to us when we get a chance to work with the Visualforce charting feature.

Using the FOR REFERENCE clause

The `FOR REFERENCE` clause is used to find the date/time when a record has been referenced. The `LastReferencedDate` field is updated for any retrieved records. The `FOR REFERENCE` clause is used to track the date/time when a record has been referenced last while executing a SOQL query.

A sample query is given as follows:

```
SELECT City__c, State__c, LastReferencedDate FROM Employee__c FOR
REFERENCE
```

When we execute the preceding query for the first time, it shows the last reference date of the record in the `LastReferencedDate` column. However, for the second time, all the records will show the same date and time (the date and time when we executed the query for the first time) for `LastReferencedDate`.

Using the FOR VIEW clause

The `FOR VIEW` clause is used to find the date when a record has been last viewed. The `LastViewedDate` field is updated for any retrieved records. The `FOR VIEW` clause is used to track the date when the record was viewed last while executing a SOQL query.

A sample query is given as follows:

```
SELECT City__c, State__c, LastViewedDate FROM Employee__c FOR VIEW
```

When we execute the preceding query for the first time, it shows the last viewed date of the record in the `LastViewedDate` column. However, for the second time, all the records will show the same date and time (the date and time when we executed the query for the first time) for `LastViewedDate`.

Using the GROUP BY CUBE clause

The `GROUP BY CUBE` clause is used to add subtotals for every possible combination of the grouped field in the query results. The `GROUP BY CUBE` clause can be used with aggregate functions such as `SUM()` and `COUNT(fieldName)`. A SOQL query with a `GROUP BY CUBE` clause retrieves the same aggregated records as an equivalent query with a `GROUP BY` clause. It also retrieves additional subtotal rows for each combination of fields specified in the comma-separated grouping list as well as the grand total.

A sample query is given as follows:

```
SELECT City__c, State__c, GROUPING(City__c) CityGroup, GROUPING(State__c)
StateGroup, COUNT(Id) IdCount FROM Employee__c GROUP BY CUBE(City__c,
State__c)
```

The following screenshot shows the output of the SOQL execution:

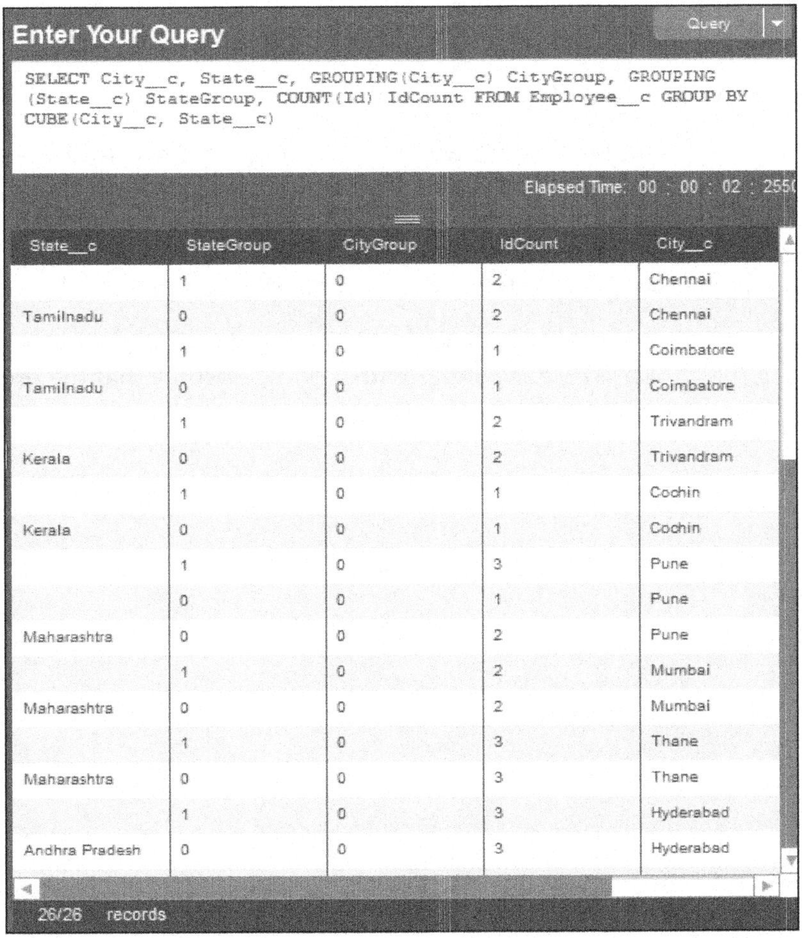

State__c	StateGroup	CityGroup	IdCount	City__c
	1	0	2	Chennai
Tamilnadu	0	0	2	Chennai
	1	0	1	Coimbatore
Tamilnadu	0	0	1	Coimbatore
	1	0	2	Trivandram
Kerala	0	0	2	Trivandram
	1	0	1	Cochin
Kerala	0	0	1	Cochin
	1	0	3	Pune
	0	0	1	Pune
Maharashtra	0	0	2	Pune
	1	0	2	Mumbai
Maharashtra	0	0	2	Mumbai
	1	0	3	Thane
Maharashtra	0	0	3	Thane
	1	0	3	Hyderabad
Andhra Pradesh	0	0	3	Hyderabad

Using the OFFSET clause

The `OFFSET` clause is used to specify the starting row number from which the records will be fetched. The `OFFSET` clause will be very useful when we implement pagination in the Visualforce page. The `OFFSET` clause along with `LIMIT` is very useful in retrieving a subset of the records. The `OFFSET` usage in SOQL has many limitations and restrictions. The limitation and guidelines for using `OFFSET` will be discussed in detail in *Chapter 5, Limitations and Best Practices*.

A sample query is given as follows:

```
SELECT Name FROM Account OFFSET 100
```

The preceding query will fetch all the accounts starting from the row number `101`. The first 100 records will not be fetched.

Let us see an example for `OFFSET` along with `LIMIT`.

A sample query is given as follows:

```
SELECT Name FROM Account OFFSET 100 LIMIT 50
```

The preceding query will fetch all the accounts starting from row number `101` to `150`. Only these 50 records will be fetched. The `OFFSET` clause along with `LIMIT` helps to create the pagination concept in the Visualforce page very easily. The offset calculation is done on the server side. So, we have to be very careful when implementing pagination since it fetches fresh data for each query call.

Salesforce.com recommends that we use the `ORDER BY` clause whenever we use `OFFSET`. Using the `ORDER BY` clause along with `OFFSET` ensures that the ordering of the result set is consistent.

Summary

In this chapter, we saw how to query the records from more than one object using the relationship queries. The steps to get the relationship name among objects were also provided. Querying the records using both standard relationship and custom relationship was also discussed.

Filtering multiselect picklist field values using the `INCLUDES` and `EXCLUDES` operators was explained. The grouping of records using `GROUP BY ROLLUP` and `GROUP BY CUBE` were also discussed.

To find the last viewed date of the record and to find the last referenced date of the record using `FOR VIEW` and `FOR REFERENCE`, respectively, were also explained. We also discussed pagination in the Visualforce page using `OFFSET` and `LIMIT`.

The next chapter deals with the functions that are available in SOQL. The functions help us to reuse the commands instead of writing conditions again and again.

4
Functions in SOQL

SOQL has many built-in functions to perform manipulations using the retrieved data. This chapter deals with the usage of functions in SOQL. We will learn how these functions of SOQL reduce and avoid the usage of long SOQL statements. It is mainly used to simplify complex SOQL statements. These functions can just be called to perform repeated tasks.

Summarizing the records using the `GROUP BY` clause will also be explained with real-time examples. We will also explain all the aggregated functions and discuss how to filter the aggregated values using the `HAVING` clause.

Using the toLabel() method

The `toLabel()` method is used to convert the results of a particular field into the user's language. All organizations can use `toLabel()`. The `toLabel()` method is of great help to an organization whose **Translation Workbench** is enabled.

The `toLabel()` method is used to get the translated values. The translation will be done on the user's locale who is querying the records.

There are many limitations of using `toLabel()`. These limitations are discussed in detail in *Chapter 5, Limitations and Best Practices*. Keep these limitations while in mind using `toLabel()`.

> The Translation Workbench is used to specify all the languages in which the configurations performed in your organization can be translated.

A sample query is given as follows:

```
SELECT Name, toLabel(Industry) FROM Account
```

The preceding query retrieves all the records from the `Account` object whose `Industry` field values will be displayed in the querying user's locale. The following screenshot shows us the output of the SOQL execution:

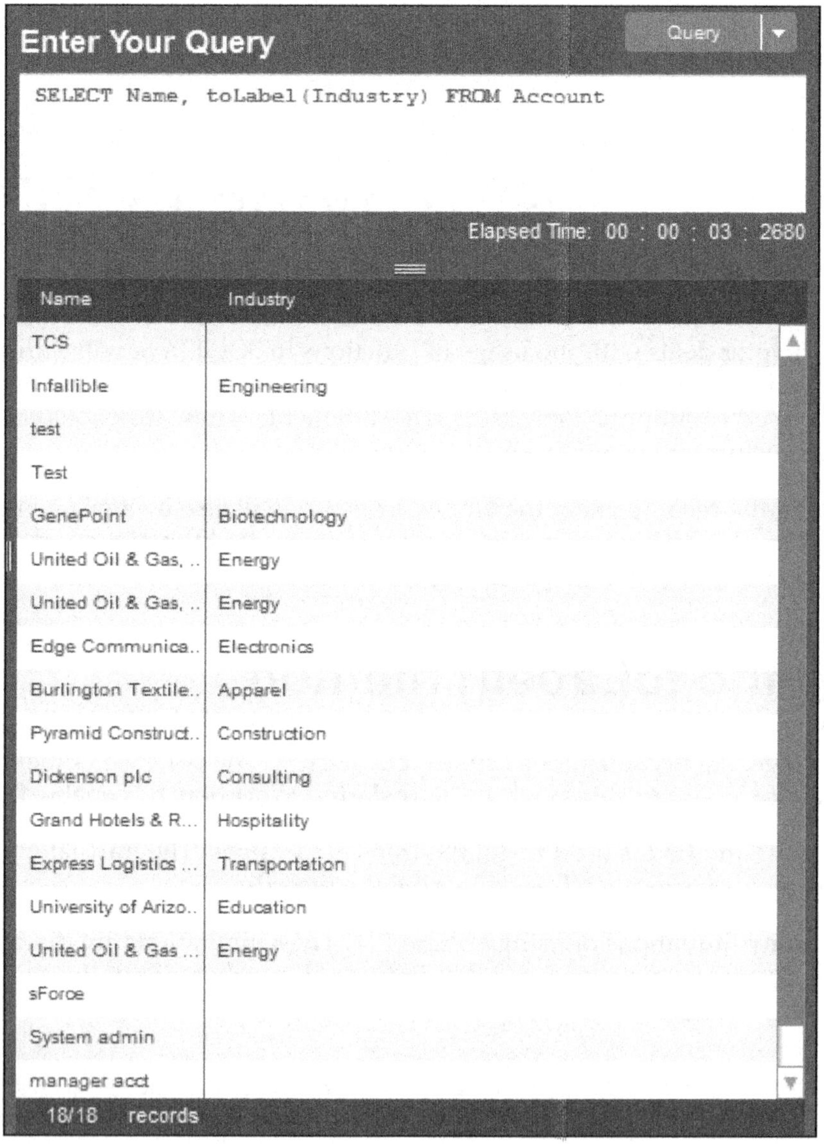

The output of the query shows us the `Name` and `Industry` column in the querying user's locale. If the `Industry` values were in different languages, we would have been able to see those values in the current user's locale. Organizations that have the Translation Workbench enabled can effectively make use of this feature.

Using the GROUP BY clause

So far, all the queries that we saw were used to retrieve the records that match the WHERE conditions. We can also summarize our records using the GROUP BY clause.

The GROUP BY clause is used to group the set of records by the values specified in the field. The GROUP BY clause will gather all of the records that contain data in the specified fields together and will allow aggregate functions to be performed on one or more fields.

The GROUP BY clause is used along with the aggregate functions to group the retrieved records using one or more fields. We can use a GROUP BY clause without an aggregated function to query all the distinct values, including the null values for an object. In order to avoid null values, COUNT_DISTINCT() is used. The COUNT_DISTINCT() usage is further discussed later.

The aggregate functions available in SOQL are as follows:

- COUNT()
- COUNT(FIELD_NAME)
- COUNT_DISTINCT()
- SUM()
- MIN()
- MAX()

The preceding six aggregate functions are used along with the GROUP BY clause in SOQL to fetch our required statistical data from the objects. These aggregate functions are very useful when the requirements need summarized or grouped values.

Let's see a sample query with the COUNT(FIELD_NAME) aggregate function. All the aggregate functions are discussed in detail with examples.

A sample query is given as follows:

```
SELECT City__c, Count(Employee_Name__c) FROM Employee__c GROUP BY City__c
```

The preceding query is used to find the number of employees in each and every city. It also fetches the number of records and shows us the count of employees whose `City` column value is null or blank. The following screenshot shows us the output of the preceding query execution:

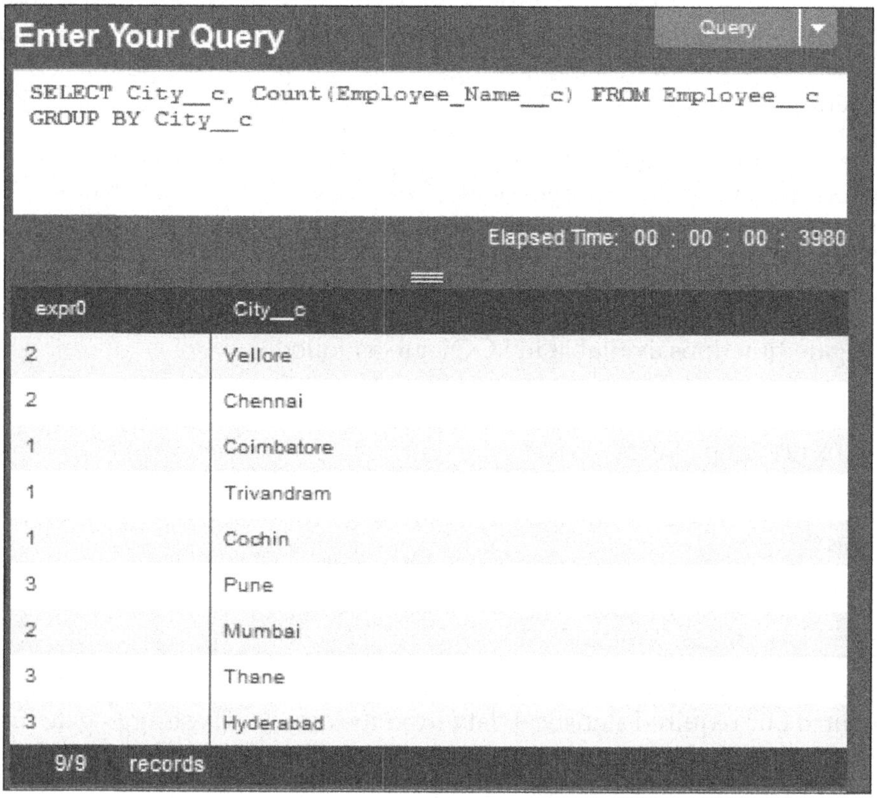

Using the COUNT() method

The `COUNT()` method is used to find the total number of records that match the specified condition. The `COUNT ()` method is also used to find the total number of records in an object. It is used to find the number of elements of a finite set of objects.

A sample query is given as follows:

```
SELECT COUNT() FROM Employee__c WHERE State__c = 'Tamilnadu'
```

Using the COUNT(Field_Name) method

The `Count(Field_Name)` method is used to find the total number of records of a particular value in the specified field. If we use `Count(Field_Name)`, it finds the total for each and every value of that field name. For example, if we use `Count(City__c)`, it will return the total number of records for each city.

The syntax of the query is given as follows:

```
SELECT COUNT(FIELD_NAME) FROM Object_API_Name
```

A sample query is given as follows:

```
SELECT City__c, Count(Employee_Name__c) FROM Employee__c GROUP BY City__c
```

The following screenshot shows us the output of the preceding query execution:

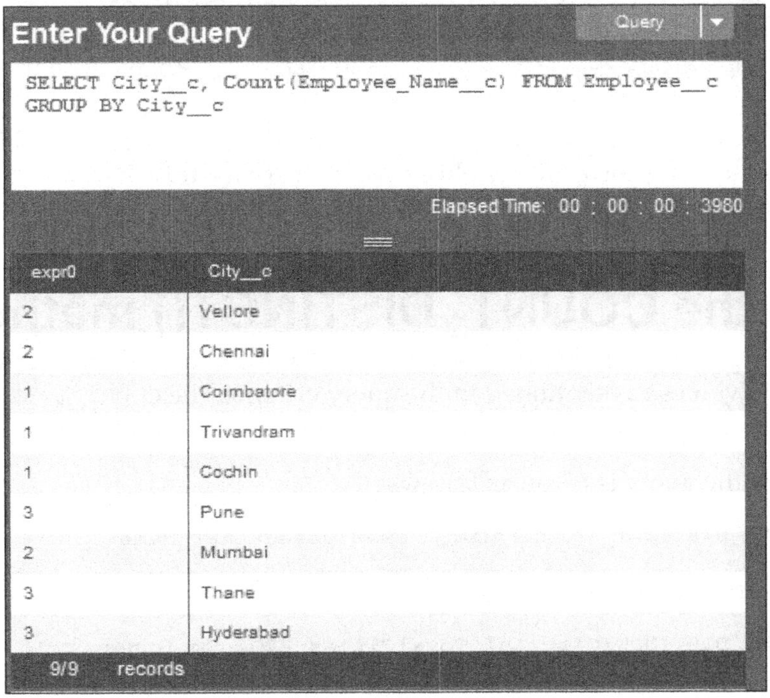

A sample query is given as follows:

```
SELECT Count(Id) TotalRecords FROM Employee__c
```

The preceding query is used to find the total number of records in an object. The following screenshot shows us the output of the preceding query execution:

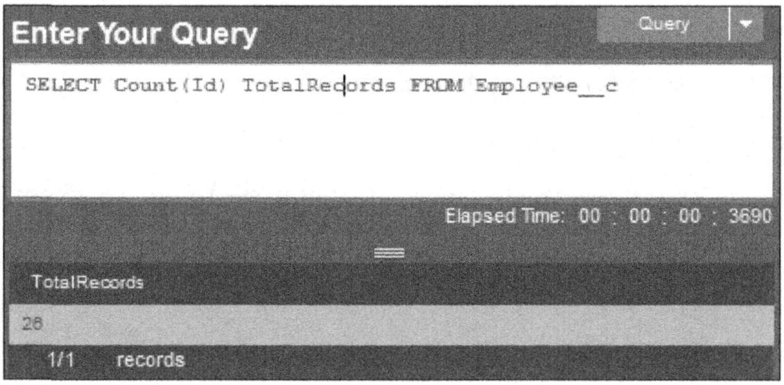

The output shows us that the total number of records in the `Employee` object is `26`. The total number of records in any object will be very useful when we create charts using the Visualforce charting.

Using the COUNT_DISTINCT() method

The `Count_DISTINCT()` method in SOQL is used to find the number of distinct non-null field values as mentioned in the query criteria. The `COUNT_DISTINCT()` method ignores the null values and returns the non-null values while querying.

The syntax of the query is given as follows:

```
SELECT COUNT_DISTINCT (FIELD_NAME) FROM Object_API_Name
```

A sample query is given as follows:

```
SELECT COUNT_DISTINCT(City__c) TotalCities FROM Employee__c
```

The preceding query is used to find the number of distinct cities the employees belong to. The following screenshot shows us the output of the preceding query execution:

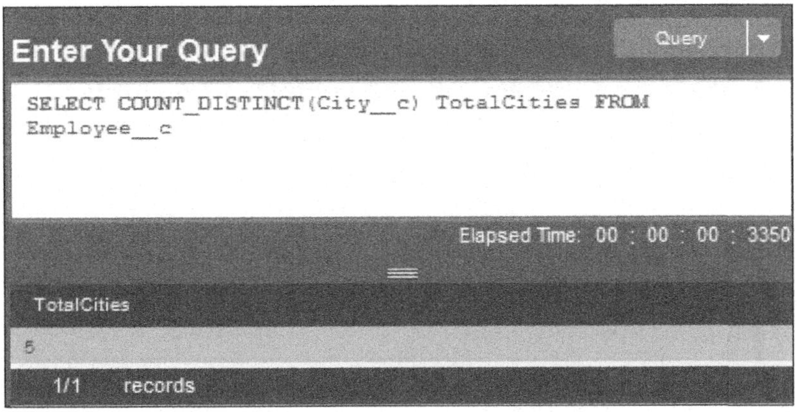

The output shows us that there are five unique or distinct cities that the employees belong to.

Using the MIN() method

The `MIN()` method in SOQL is used to return the minimum or smallest value of the mentioned field. The `MIN(x)` method is used to return the minimum value of the `x` field.

The syntax of the query is given as follows:

```
SELECT MIN (FIELD_NAME) FROM Object_API_Name
```

A sample query is given as follows:

```
SELECT MIN(Age__c) MinAge, City__c FROM Employee__c GROUP BY City__c
```

The preceding query is used to find the minimum age of an employee in each and every city. It will not show us the values of employees if their `City` values are blank or null. The following screenshot shows us the output of the preceding query execution:

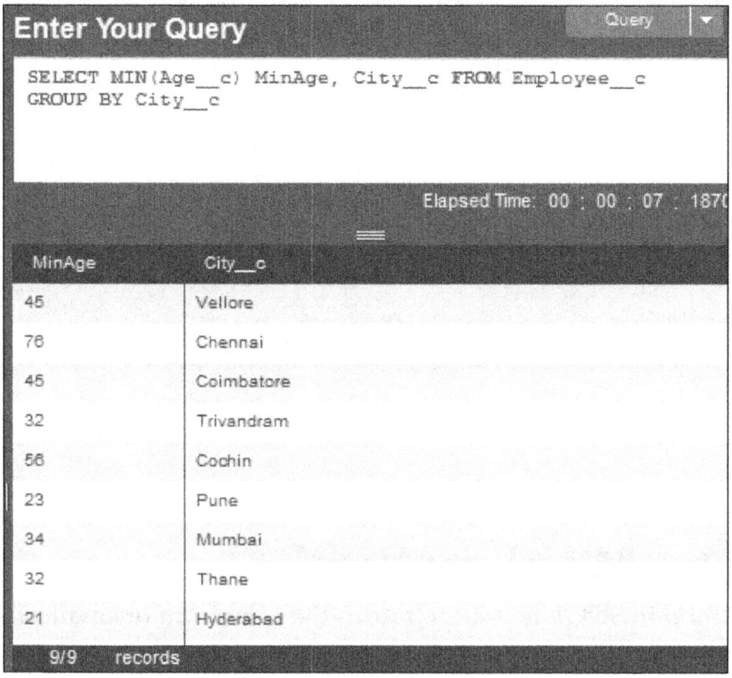

The output shows us the minimum age of an employee in a city.

Using the MAX() method

The `MAX()` method in SOQL is used to return the maximum or the largest value of the mentioned field. The `MAX(x)` method is used to return the maximum value of the `x` field.

The syntax of the query is given as follows:

```
SELECT MAX (FIELD_NAME) FROM Object_API_Name
```

A sample query is given as follows:

```
SELECT MAX(Age__c) MaxAge, City__c FROM Employee__c GROUP BY City__c
```

The preceding query is used to find the maximum age of an employee in each and every city. The following screenshot shows us the output of the preceding query execution:

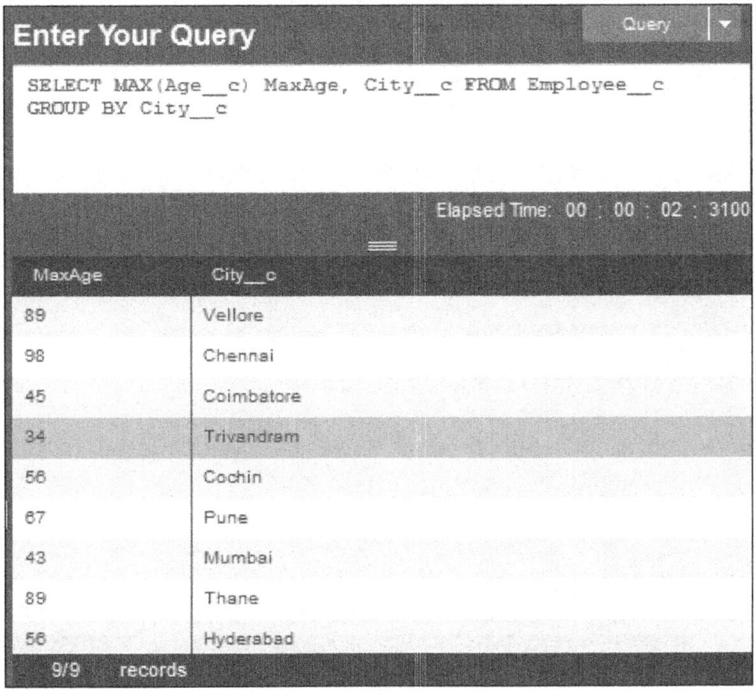

The output shows us the minimum age of an employee in a city.

Using the SUM() method

The `SUM()` method is used to find the total of the specified numeric field. The numeric fields available in Salesforce.com are `Currency`, `Percent`, and `Number`. The `SUM()` method is used to add a sequence of numeric fields. The result of `SUM()` is their sum or total.

The syntax of the query is given as follows:

```
SELECT SUM (FIELD_NAME) FROM Object_API_Name
```

A sample query is given as follows:

```
SELECT SUM(Age__c) MaxAge, City__c FROM Employee__c GROUP BY City__c
```

The preceding query returns the total age of employees in each and every city. The following screenshot shows us the output of the preceding query execution:

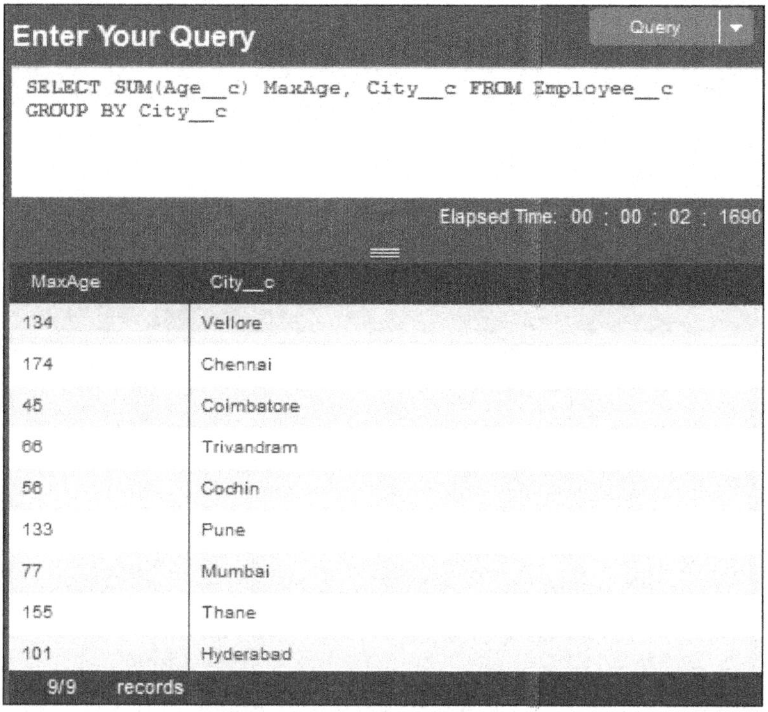

Using the HAVING clause

The `HAVING` clause is very similar to the `WHERE` clause. However, the only difference between the `HAVING` and `WHERE` clause is that the `HAVING` clause is used only with the aggregate functions.

The `HAVING` clause is used to specify the search condition in the `GROUP BY` clause or the aggregate functions. The `HAVING` clause limits the grouped records returned by a SOQL statement. However, the `WHERE` clause limits the records returned by a SOQL statement.

A `HAVING` clause in SOQL is used to specify that the SOQL `SELECT` statement should only return the records whose aggregate values meet the specified conditions.

A sample query is given as follows:

```
SELECT City__c, COUNT(Employee_Name__c) FROM Employee__c GROUP BY City__c
HAVING COUNT(City__c) >= 1
```

The following screenshot shows us the output of the preceding query execution:

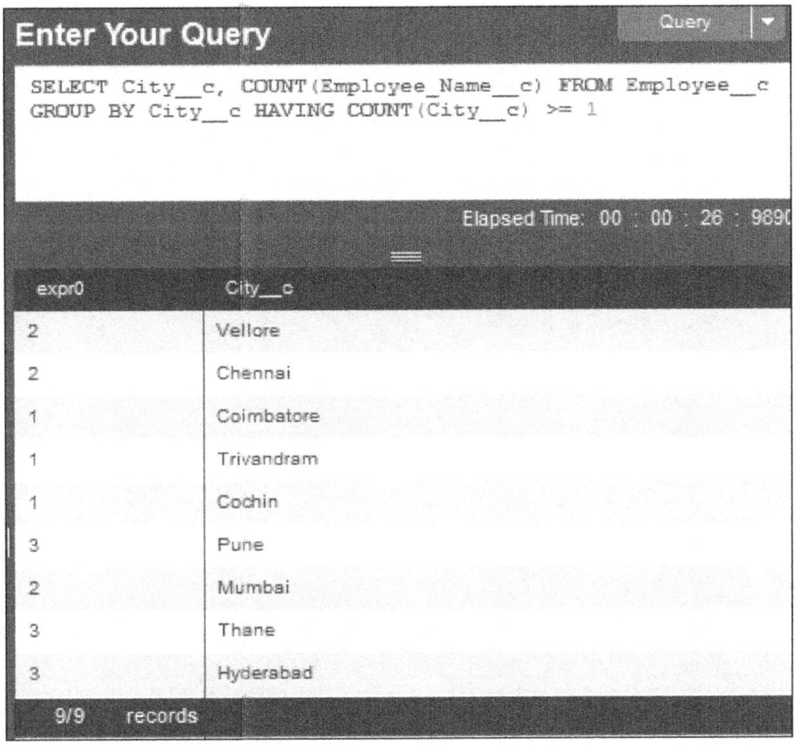

The output of the SOQL execution shows us the number of employees in each and every city whose number of records in each and every city is greater than one. This condition ignores all the employees whose `City` is null. It also ignores the employees if the number of employees in a city is less than or equal to one.

Summary

In this chapter, we learned about all the functions that are available in SOQL. We discussed the method to translate the field values using `toLabel()`, which will be very useful when we want to translate the values and show them in a report.

Grouping or summarizing the records with aggregate functions was also discussed. The six aggregate functions were discussed with the syntax and real-time examples. We also discussed the situations in which we have to use the `HAVING` and `WHERE` clauses.

5
Limitations and Best Practices

In this chapter, we will take a look at the standards and best practices to be followed by an administrator or a developer while writing SOQL statements during development and administration tasks. We will also cover the limitations that should be considered while writing the SOQL statements.

Salesforce has set many limitations as all the Apex code runs on the Apex engine. Apex is an object-oriented programming language that allows the Salesforce developers to execute flow and transaction control statements on the Force.com platform. So, whenever we write the SOQL statements, we should make sure that we do not hit the limitations set by Salesforce. All the limitations will be explained in detail.

We will also discuss in detail the limitations in `OFFSET`, `toLabel()`, `COUNT()`, and `ORDER BY` in the SOQL statements and the limitations in writing the relationship queries will.

Standards to be followed in SOQL

Let's take a look the standards to be followed in SOQL.

If we want avoid the number of records fetched from an object, we have to use the `LIMIT` option. The `LIMIT` option limits the number of records that were fetched and avoids the limits in Salesforce.

We have seen the reserved keywords in SOQL in *Chapter 1, Introduction to SOQL*. In order to differentiate between the reserved keywords in a SQOL query, always write the reserved keywords in uppercase so that it will be easy for us to identify them. Write `SELECT`, `FROM`, `WHERE`, `HAVING`, `IN`, and so on in uppercase.

If we want to use a single quote inside our SOQL statement, we will have to use a backslash followed by a single quote. This is called as an escape sequence. We are allowed to use the escape sequences in SOQL as shown in the following table:

Sequence	Description
`\n` or `\N`	New line
`\t` or `\T`	Tab
`\b` or `\B`	Bell
`\r` or `\R`	Carriage return
`\f` or `\F`	Form feed
`\"`	One double-quote character
`\\`	Backslash
`\'`	One single-quote character

A sample query is given as follows:

```
SELECT Id, Industry FROM Account WHERE Name LIKE 'Infallible Techie\'s
Company'
```

Best practices

We can use SOQL in the following situations:

- When we know the object in which we have our required data
- When we want to fetch data from multiple objects with a lookup or master-detail relationship
- When we want to have the data set in a sorted manner
- When we want to summarize the data
- When we want to limit our data while retrieving it

For indexing, the following fields can be used in SOQL:

- `Id` can be used as the primary key.
- Lookup or master-detail relationship fields can be used as the foreign key.
- The custom fields can be used as the external IDs. An external ID in Salesorce is used as unique record identifiers from a system outside of Salesforce. When you select this option, the import wizard will detect existing records in Salesforce that have the same external ID. Note that this operation is not case-sensitive. For example, `ABC` will be matched with `abc`.

  Here, `Id` is the record ID that is autogenerated whenever a new record is created. The record ID of Salesforce represents a unique record within a Salesforce instance. There are two versions of every record ID in Salesforce. They are as follows:

  - A 15-digit case-sensitive version, which is referenced in the user interface
  - An 18-digit case-insensitive version, which is referenced through the API

Fields that can't be indexed in SOQL are as follows:

- Multiselect picklists
- The `Currency` fields in a multicurrency organization
- The long text fields
- Some formula fields
- The binary fields (fields of the type blob, file, or encrypted text)

Limitations in objects

An object represents database tables that contain your organization's information. Objects in Salesforce are mainly used to store records. There are two types of objects in Salesforce: standard objects and custom objects. Salesforce-defined objects are the standard objects, and the objects created by a user in an organization are the custom objects. While writing the SOQL statements to fetch records from the objects shown in the following table, we have to check the limits set by Salesforce:

Object	Limits in SOQL
ContentDocumentLink	In the ContentDocumentLink object, a SOQL query must filter on one of the Id, ContentDocumentId, or LinkedEntityId objects.
NewsFeed	In the NewsFeed object, the SOQL ORDER BY clause on the fields using relationships is not available.
KnowledgeArticleVersion	The archived article versions are stored in the articletype_kav object. To query the archived article versions, specify the article Id and setsLatestVersion='0'.
UserRecordAccess	In the UserRecordAccess object, the maximum number of records that can be queried is 200.
UserProfileFeed	In the UserProfileFeed object, the SOQL ORDER BY clause on the fields using relationships is not available. A query must include WITH UserId = {userId].

Other limitations

The following sections cover the limitations in the objects, apart from those mentioned in the preceding section.

Governor limits

As Apex runs in a multitenant environment, the Apex runtime engine strictly enforces a number of limits to ensure that the runaway Apex doesn't monopolize the shared resources. If some Apex code ever exceeds a limit, the associated governor issues a runtime exception that cannot be handled. The governor limits in the following table are subject to change, so use the following link to get the latest information:

`http://www.salesforce.com/us/developer/docs/apexcode/Content/apex_gov_limits.htm`

Query usage	Limitation
The total number of SOQL queries issued	100
The total number of SOQL queries issued for the Apex batch and future methods	200
The total number of records retrieved by the SOQL queries	50,000
The total number of records retrieved by `Database.getQueryLocator`	10,000

If a SOQL query runs for more than 120 seconds, the request can be canceled by Salesforce.

Understanding the limitations of the ORDER BY query

The limitations of the `ORDER BY` query are as follows:

- The data types that are not supported in `ORDER BY` are reference, multiselect picklists, and long text area.
- We can use `ORDER BY` with the optional `LIMIT` option in a `SELECT` statement.
- We are limited to using 32 fields in an `ORDER BY` SOQL query. If we exceed this limit, malformed query fault information is returned.

Understanding the limitations of the toLabel() query

The limitations of the `toLabel()` query are as follows:

- The `toLabel()` method cannot be used along with `ORDER BY` in a SOQL
- We cannot use `toLabel()` in the `WHERE` clause for the division or currency ISO code picklists

Understanding the limitations of the COUNT() query

The limitations of the `COUNT` query are as follows:

- The `COUNT()` query cannot be used with other elements in the `SELECT` list.
- We cannot use `COUNT()` with an `ORDER BY` clause. The option for this is `COUNT(fieldname)`.
- We cannot use `COUNT()` with a `GROUP BY` clause for the API Version 19.0 and higher. The option for this is `COUNT(fieldName)`.

Understanding the limitations of the OFFSET clause

The limitations of the OFFSET clause are as follows:

- The maximum `OFFSET` limit is 2,000 rows. If we set an `OFFSET` limit higher than 2,000, we will get the result in a `NUMBER_OUTSIDE_VALID_RANGE` error.
- The `OFFSET` clause is mainly focused to be used in a top-level query, and it is not allowed in most of the subqueries.
- The `OFFSET` clause is allowed in the SOQL that is used in SOAP API, REST API, and Apex. It's not allowed in SOQL used within bulk API or streaming API.

Limitations of the relationship queries

The limitations of the relationship queries are as follows:

- Objects should have a relationship between them to write relationship queries. We cannot write relationship queries if the objects don't have any relationship between them.
- We cannot write more than 35 child-to-parent relationships in a SOQL statement.
- We cannot write more than 20 parent-to-child relationships in a SOQL statement.
- In each specified relationship between objects, no more than five levels can be specified in a child-to-parent relationship.

- In each specified relationship among objects, only one level of a parent-to-child relationship can be specified in a query.
- For custom relationships, `__r` should be mandatorily added at the end of the relationship name.

Notes and Attachments limitations

The limitations of the `Notes` and `Attachments` objects are as follows:

- The `Notes` and `Attachments` objects cannot be filtered with the help of the content or body. It can be filtered only with `Name`, `CreatedDate`, and so on.
- The `Notes` and `Attachments` objects are not supported in the subquery.

Summary

In this chapter, we saw the standards to be followed while writing the SOQL statements. The best practices explained in this chapter allow us to retrieve the required records by properly filtering the data. As a developer or an administrator, we should follow these standards and best practices.

Whenever we write SOQL statements to fetch the data, we should be very careful about the limitations. The different limitations with the objects are to be considered while writing the SOQL statements to fetch data from the objects. The other limitations with `OFFSET`, `ORDER BY`, `COUNT()`, `toLabel()`, and governor limits should also be considered while writing the SOQL statements with these functions.

In the next chapter, we are going to take a look at the recommended installation guidelines to be followed while installing the tools for the SOQL statement execution. These tools will help us execute all the queries that we have discussed so far.

6

Tools with Installation Guidelines

We need some tools in order to execute SOQL statements. This chapter deals with the installation guidelines of some of the tools that are available. This chapter covers some basic tips that we can use during the installation of tools. It provides everything you need to complete the installation, from initial setup to the final SOQL execution. The chapter focuses on tools software and covers all recommended guidelines to be followed.

Using the Force.com Explorer software

Using the Force.com Explorer software, we can build and test our SOQL queries. It also allows us to export the queried data in the **Comma Separated Value** (**CSV**) format. It's an AIR application. So, you need to install Adobe AIR before installing it. The Force.com Explorer software is mainly used for a smaller set of records. It cannot be used for bulk operations. For bulk operations, **Apex Data Loader** is the best tool.

We can edit and delete records using the Force.com Explorer software.

Installing Force.com Explorer

The steps to install the Force.com Explorer software are as follows:

1. Go to `http://wiki.developerforce.com/page/ForceExplorer`.

2. Install **Adobe Air** first and then **Force.com Explorer**. Without installing Adobe AIR, we will not be able to open the Force.com Explorer AIR file, as shown in the following screenshot:

3. Open the **Force.com Explorer** window using the shortcut menu on the desktop or from the **Start** menu.
4. Enter your **Username, Password, and Security Token** (in case you are accessing from outside IP ranges).

5. Select an **Environment** (**Production** or **Sandbox**) option in **Advanced Options** as shown in the following screenshot:

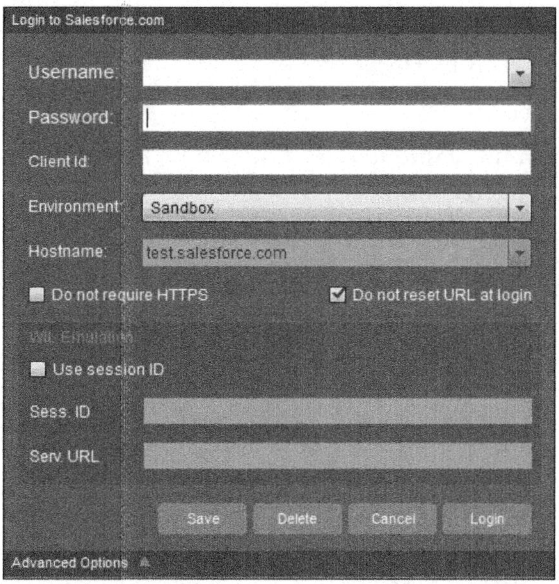

6. Click on the **Login** button.
7. Build your query and click on the **Query** button to view the result as shown in the following screenshot:

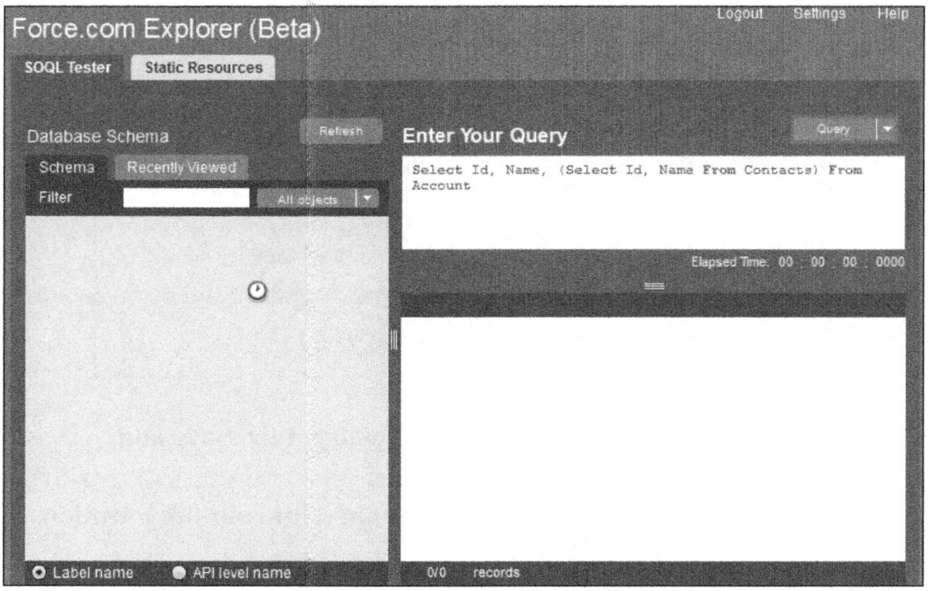

The Force.com Explorer also lists the static resources used in our Salesforce.com organization.

To update the record using Force.com Explorer, perform the following steps:

1. Log in to Force.com Explorer.
2. Query some records.
3. Double-click on the value to edit it. It will be highlighted as shown in the following screenshot:

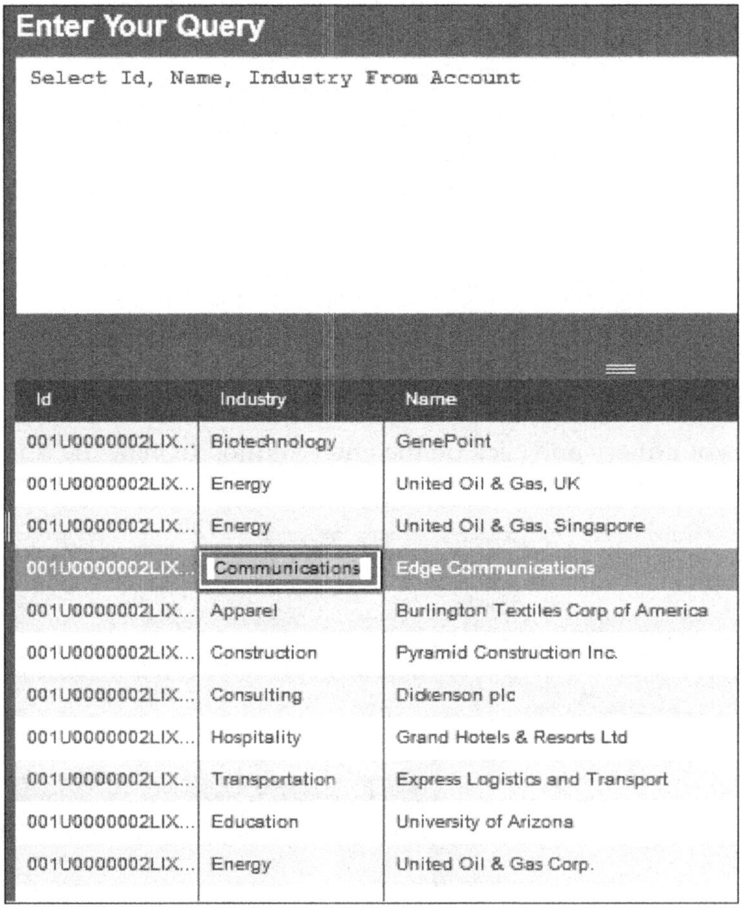

4. Enter the new value and press *Enter*; you will get the **Save** and **Cancel** options.
5. Click on **Save** to update the new value entered into our organization.

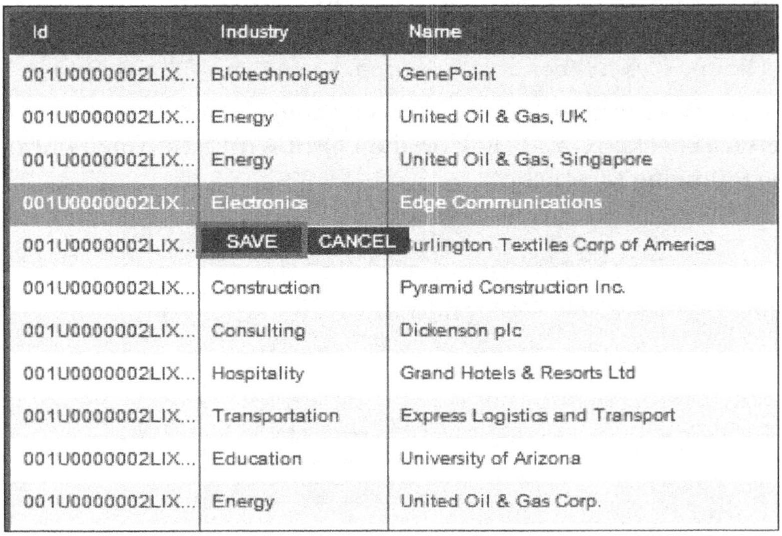

6. You will get an alert message showing whether the record has been saved successfully. Click on **OK** to resume. Refer to the following screenshot:

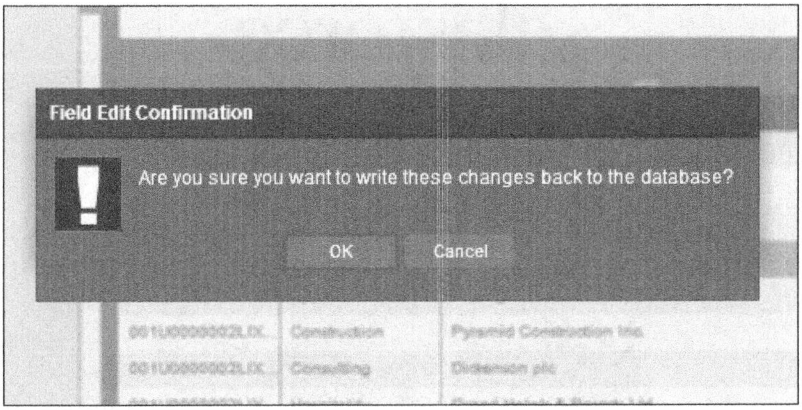

Workbench

Workbench is a simple web-based tool that is very useful for Salesforce administrators and developers to interact with Salesforce organizations via the Force.com APIs. Workbench allows us to execute **Salesforce Object Search Language** (**SOSL**). Unlike SOQL, which can only query one object at a time and multiple objects only if they have a relationship, SOSL enables you to search text, e-mail, and phone fields for multiple objects simultaneously.

To get started with Workbench, perform the following steps:

1. Go to `https://workbench.developerforce.com/login.php`.
2. Select an **Environment** option, **API Version**, check the **I agree to the terms of service** checkbox, and click on the **Login with Salesforce** button as shown in the following screenshot:

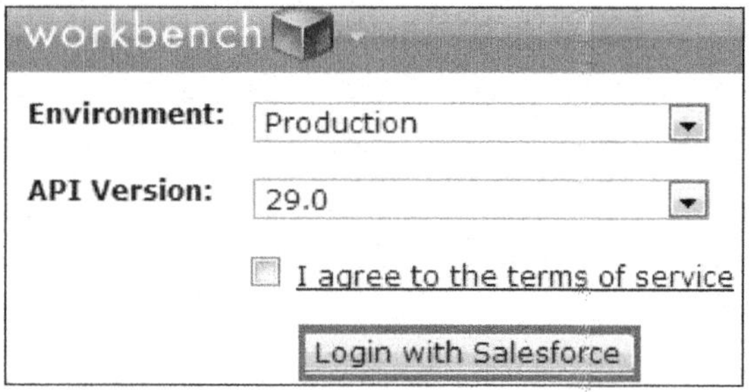

3. Enter your username and password and click on the **Log in to Salesforce** button as shown in the following screenshot:

4. Click on the **Allow** button as shown in the following screenshot:

5. Enter your query and click on the **Query** button, as shown in the following screenshot, to view the result:

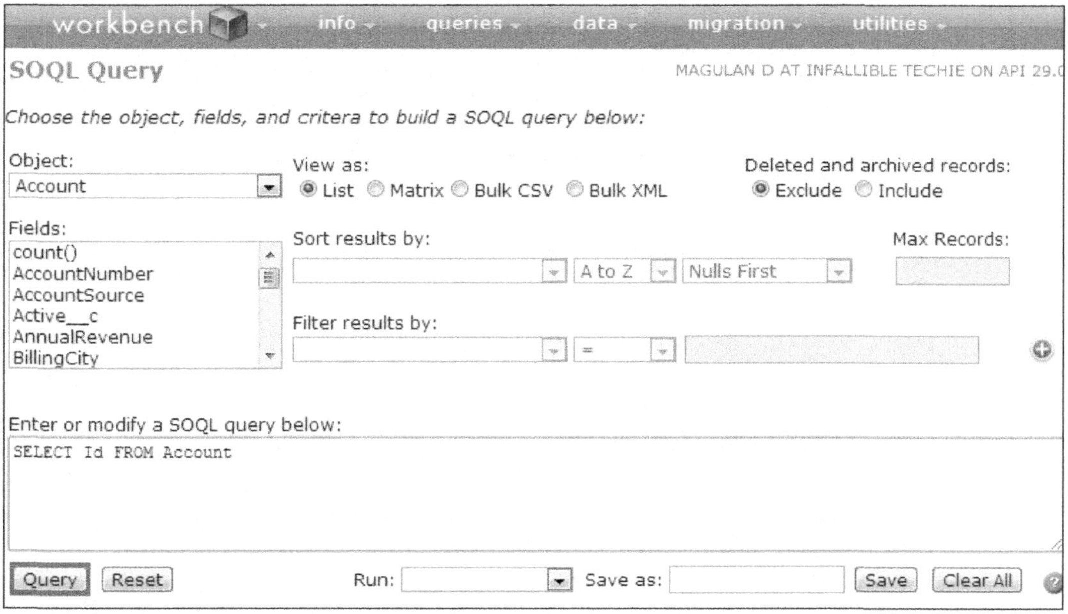

Parent-child relationship queries are not supported in Workbench before setting them first. Perform the following steps to enable parent-child relationship queries in Workbench:

1. Navigate to the **Settings** tab of Workbench as shown in the following screenshot:

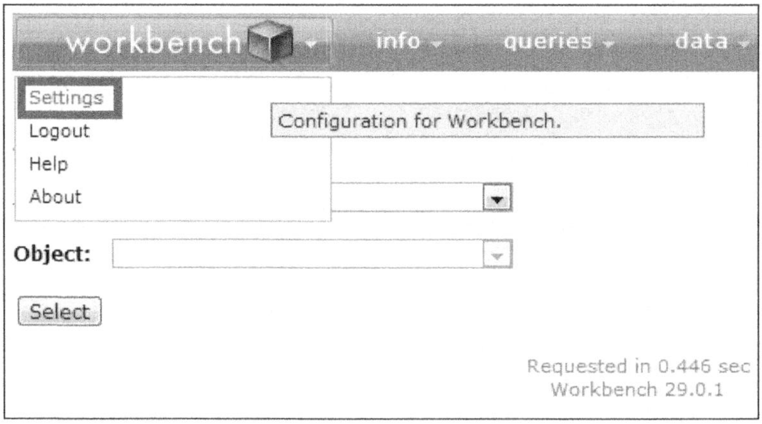

2. In **Query & Search Options**, check the **Allows SOQL Parent Relationship Queries** checkbox and click on **Apply Settings** as shown in the following screenshot:

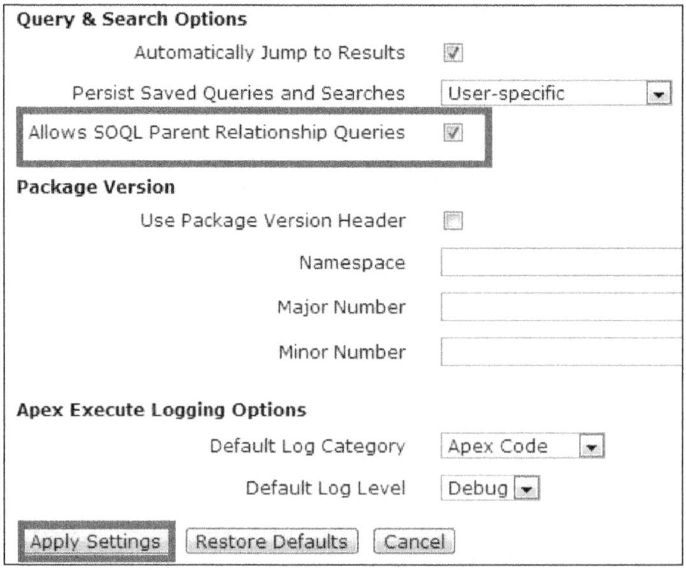

3. Now we will be able to access the parent relationship queries.

Dataloader.io

Use `Dataloader.io` to import, export, and delete data from Salesforce. Everything is online in Data Loader. There will be no software hassle if we use `Dataloader.io`. A browser and an Internet connection are more than enough to use this feature provided by a third party. It is not a Salesforce tool.

To use `Dataloader.io`, perform the following steps:

1. Go to `https://dataloader.io/`.
2. Click on the **Login with Salesforce** button.
3. Select an **Environment** option and click on the **Login** button as shown in the following screenshot:

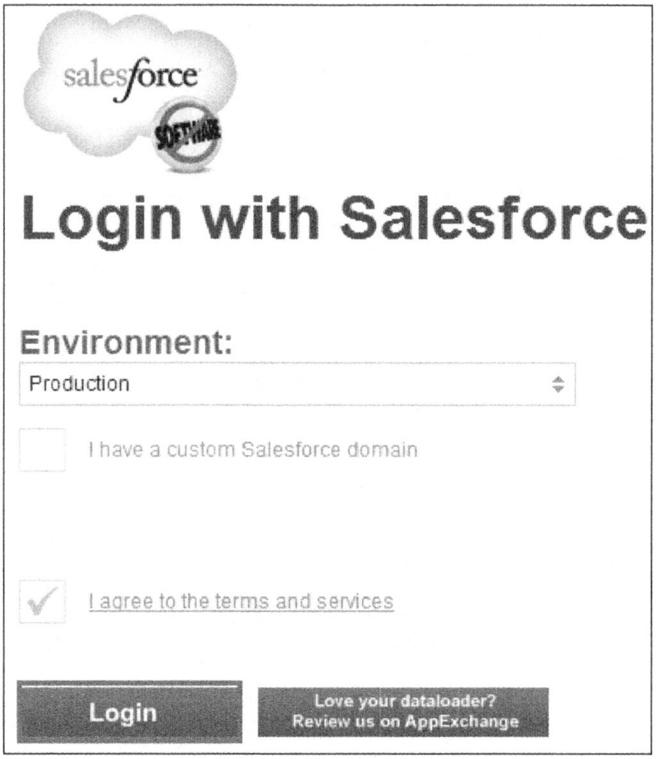

4. Enter your username and password and click on the **Log in to Salesforce** button as shown in the following screenshot:

5. Select **Export** under **New Task** as shown in the following screenshot:

6. Select **Object** and click on the **Next** button as shown in the following screenshot:

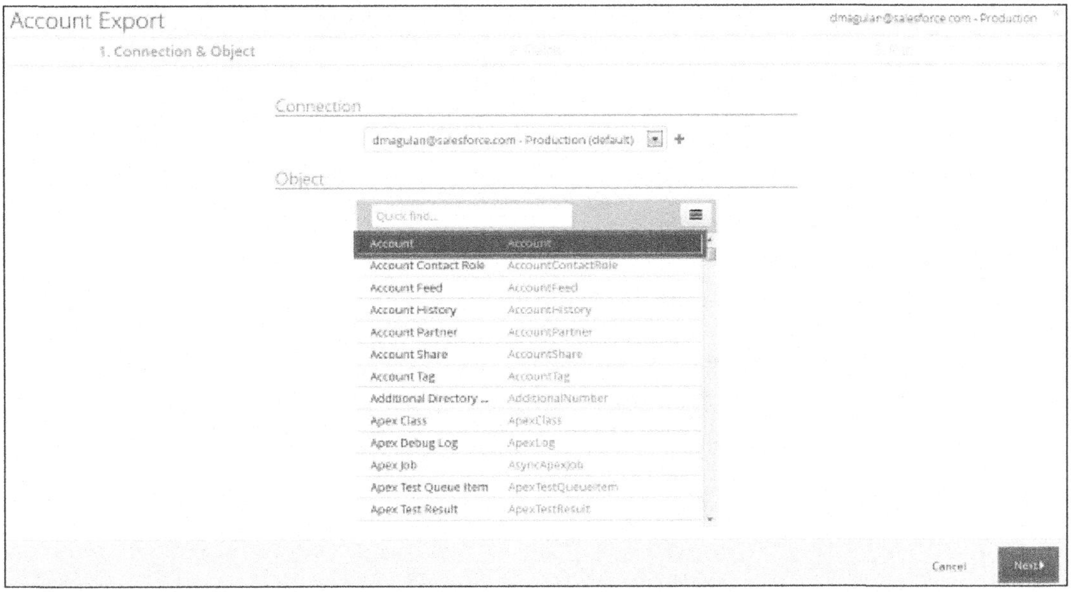

7. Select the fields and build your SOQL query; click on the **Verify** button to verify your query and then click on the **Next** button as shown in the following screenshot:

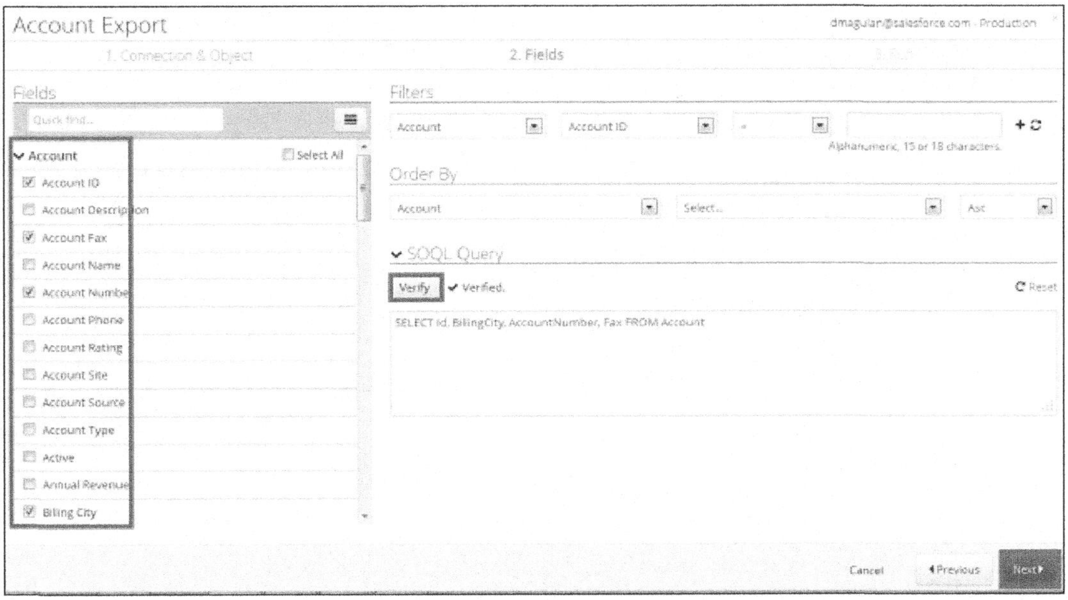

8. Schedule or run the query to be exported. Refer to the following screenshot:

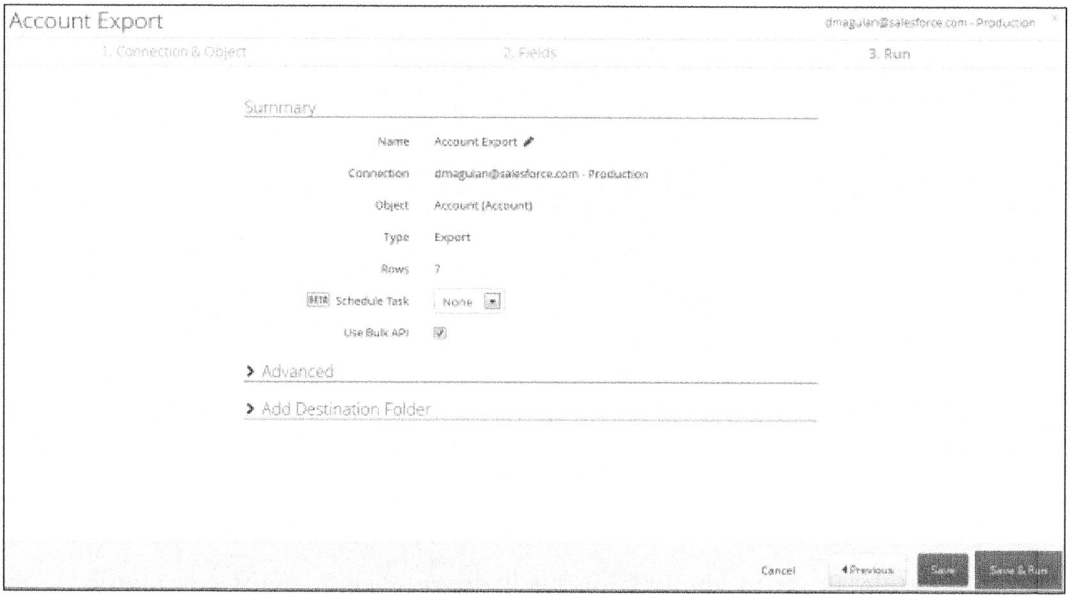

9. After execution, it shows the successfully extracted records. Refer to the following screenshot:

10. We can open this file at any time by logging in to `Dataloader.io`. Refer to the following screenshot:

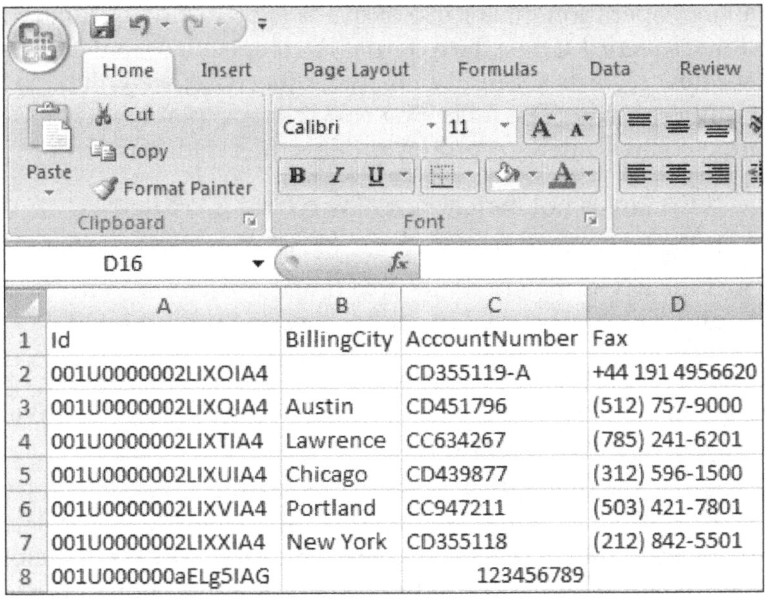

The Apex Data Loader tool

The Data Loader tool is used to export, update, insert, and delete records. It's mainly used for bulk operations.

The operations that can be performed using Apex Data Loader are as follows:

- `Insert`: On using this operation, we can insert new records into our Salesforce organization.
- `Update`: On using this operation, we can update existing records in our Salesforce organization.
- `Upsert`: On using this operation, we can insert new records into our Salesforce organization and update existing records in our Salesforce organization; in other words, `Upsert` is a combination of `Insert` and `Update`.

The `Upsert` operation makes use of the `Object` record's primary key (Salesforce's record ID) or the external ID, if specified, to determine whether new records should be created; otherwise, we will have to update the existing records . The following conditions explain when the `Upsert` operation creates a new record or updates the existing record:

  - If the key is not matched, a new record is created
  - If the key is matched once, the existing record is updated
  - If the key is matched multiple times, an error is generated and the object record is neither inserted nor updated

- `Delete`: On using the `Delete` operation, we can delete existing records from our Salesforce organization. The deleted records will be available in the Recycle Bin for 15 days.
- `Hard Delete`: On using the `Hard Delete` operation, we can delete existing records from our Salesforce organization permanently. The deleted records will not be available in the Recycle Bin. The **Bulk API Hard Delete** checkbox should be enabled, as shown in the following screenshot, in the user profile for permanently deleting records:

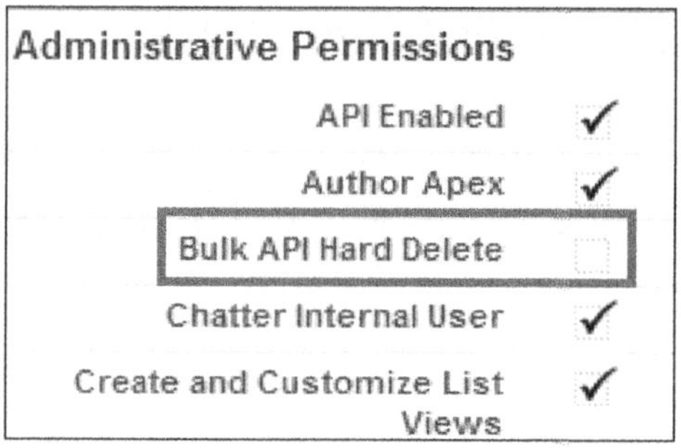

- `Export`: On using this operation, we can extract data from our Salesforce organization.
- `Export All`: On using this operation, we can extract data from our Salesforce organization. The extracted data contains the records from the **Recycle Bin** too, that is, soft-deleted records will be extracted.

The system requirements for installing Apex Data Loader are as follows:

- Microsoft Windows 7 or Windows XP
- 120 MB free disk space
- 256 MB available memory
- Java JRE 1.6 or later (Windows 7 or Windows XP)

- Sun JVM 1.6 or later (Windows 7 or Windows XP)
- Administrator privileges on the machine

To download the data loader, navigate to **Administer** | **Data Management** | **Data Loader** as shown in the following screenshot:

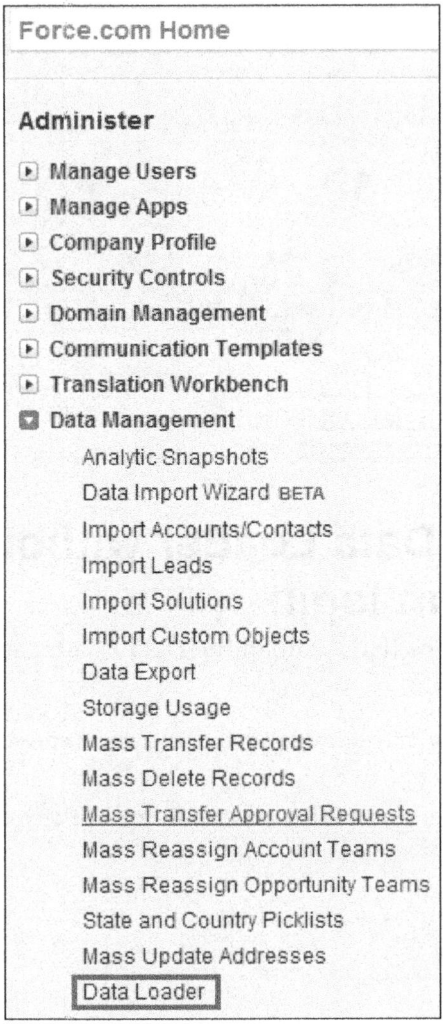

Click on the **Download the Data Loader** link as shown in the following screenshot to download Apex Data Loader:

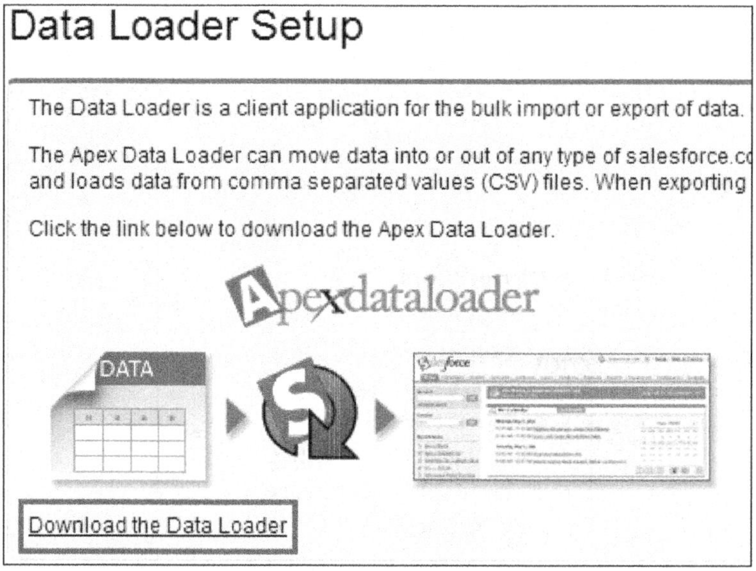

Downloading Data Loader without the Salesforce.com login

Perform the following steps to download the Data Loader setup without a Salesforce.com login:

1. Go to `http://www.cloudsuccess.com/resource-centre/apex-data-loader-archive/`.
2. Select the latest version to download. Refer to the following screenshot:

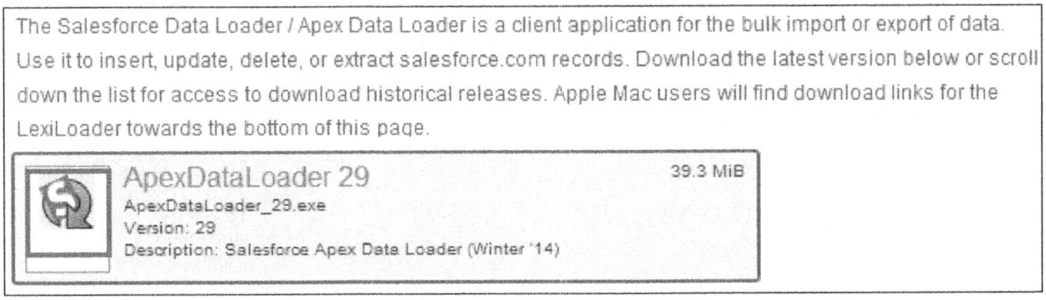

The steps for installation are as follows:

1. Double-click on the downloaded file to launch the installation wizard.
2. Click on the **Next** button.
3. Accept the license agreement and click on the **Next** button.
4. Accept the default installation directory or click on **Change...** to choose another directory. Click on the **Next** button.
5. Click on the **Install** button.
6. Click on the **Finish** button.

To start using Apex Data Loader, perform the following steps:

1. Install Apex Data Loader.
2. Open Apex Data Loader.
3. Click on the **Export** button as shown in the following screenshot:

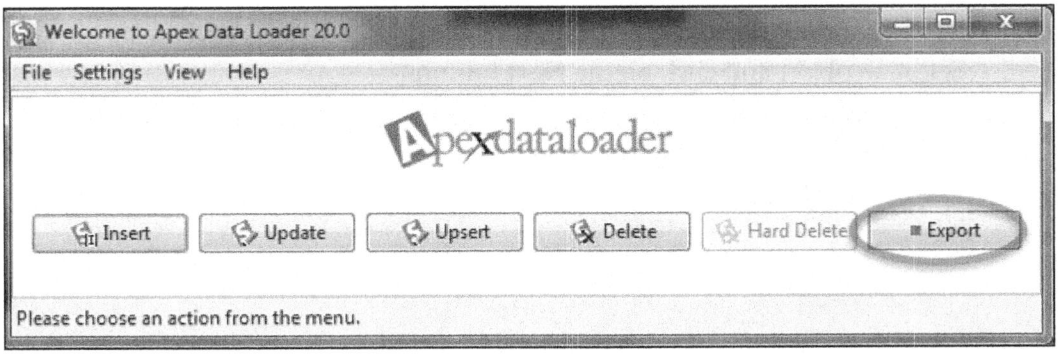

4. Enter your username, password, and security token (in case you are accessing outside the IP ranges). Click on the **Login** button. Once login is successfully completed, click on the **Next** button as shown in the following screenshot:

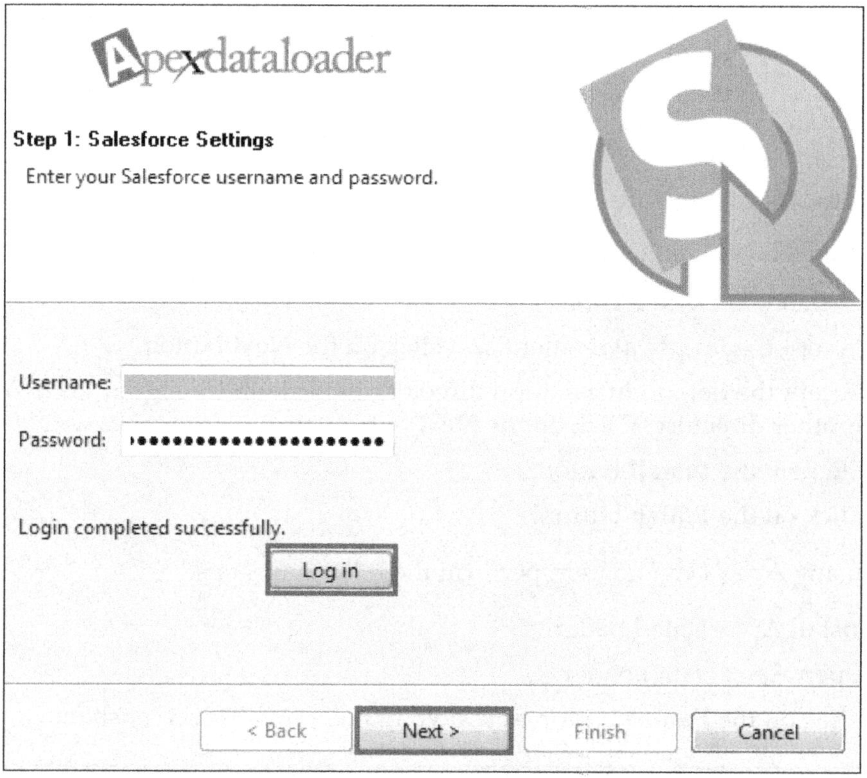

5. Select an object and click on the **Next** button.
6. Build your query to fetch the required data. We can filter the records to be fetched using the filter logic available.
7. Click on the **Next** button.

8. Click on the **Finish** button to extract the data as shown in the following screenshot:

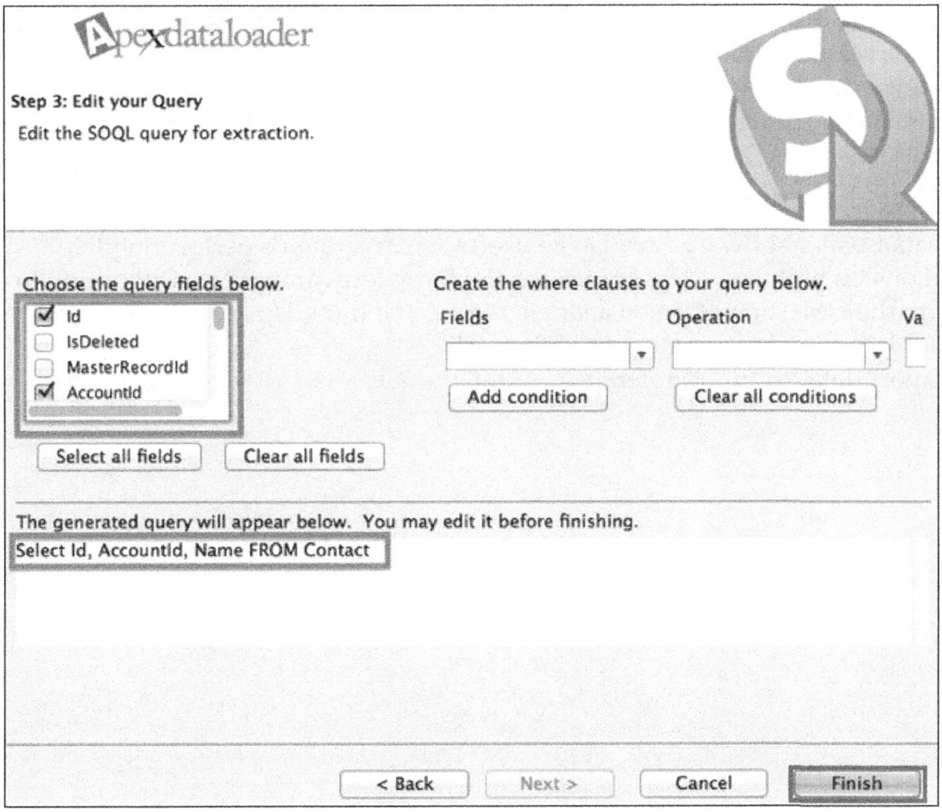

9. The exported data will be in CSV format. We can use Excel to open the extracted file.
10. It also has a built-in CSV format file viewer to view the extracted records.

Summary

In this chapter, we came to know about many applications that are available for querying records from Salesforce objects using SOQL. The step-by-step installation guide helps avoid problems during installation. These are free versions of software and a few other software options are provided by `Salesforce.com` for free. These recommended guidelines help practitioners to install the software by choosing the appropriate setups. These software are also used for data migration from legacy systems to Salesforce.

The Data Loader software can also be used for extracting or performing DML operations on bulk data. The Force.com Explorer software gives us an option to perform the DML operation on a single record at a time. This software is mainly used for handling lesser amounts of data. The `Dataloader.io` tool allows us to save and export data for future reference, and it also allows us to schedule export jobs.

Review Questions

This appendix lists the review questions of all the chapters, which will help us to recap all the chapters.

Chapter 1

The following set of questions has multiple options. Choose the number that corresponds with your answer:

Q1. SOQL stands for ...

1. Structure Object Query Language
2. Salesforce Object Query Language
3. Both 1 and 2
4. None of the above

Q2. Using `Order By`, which of the following options are true (select two)?

1. Arrange in ascending order
2. Arrange in descending order
3. Descending order is the default
4. `Order By` is not supported

Q3. Custom objects always end with `__r`.

1. True
2. False

Q4. API names of the fields should be used in SOQL instead of the label of the field.

1. True
2. False

The answers for the preceding review questions are as follows:

Q1 – 2

Q2 – 1 and 2

Q3 – 2

Q4 – 1

Chapter 2

Q1. The Alias notation in SOQL changes the label name of the field.

1. True
2. False

Q2. Select the comparison operators (select two).

1. `AND`
2. `OR`
3. `>`
4. `=`

Q3. The `INCLUDES` and `EXCLUDES` operators are used for filtering...

1. Multiselect picklists
2. Lookup
3. Master-detail
4. Many-to-many

The answers for the preceding review questions are as follows:

Q1 – 2

Q2 – 3 and 4

Q3 – 1

Chapter 3

Q1. Which operators are used to filter the multiselect picklist field in Salesforce.com?

1. `INCLUDES`
2. `EXCLUDES`
3. Both
4. None

Q2. It is possible to sort records in both ascending and descending order together in a SOQL query.

1. True
2. False

Q3. `FOR VIEW` is used to update...

1. `LastReferencedDate`
2. `LastViewedDate`
3. `LastModifiedDate`
4. `LastCreatedDate`

Q4. `FOR REFERENCE` is used to update...

1. `LastReferencedDate`
2. `LastViewedDate`
3. `LastModifiedDate`
4. `LastCreatedDate`

The answers for the preceding review questions are as follows:

Q1 - 3

Q2 - 1

Q3 - 2

Q4 - 1

Chapter 4

Q1. Which method in SOQL returns the number of distinct non-null field values?

1. `COUNT_DISTINCT()`
2. `MIN()`
3. `MAX()`
4. `COUNT()`

Q2. Which method in SOQL returns the maximum value of a field?

1. `COUNT_DISTINCT()`
2. `MIN()`
3. `MAX()`
4. `COUNT()`

Q3. Which method in SOQL returns the minimum value of a field?

1. `COUNT_DISTINCT()`
2. `MIN()`
3. `MAX()`
4. `COUNT()`

Q4. Which method in SOQL returns the total value of a field?

1. `SUM()`
2. `MIN()`
3. `MAX()`
4. `COUNT()`

Q5. Which method in SOQL returns the total number of records in an object?

1. `COUNT()`
2. `MIN()`
3. `MAX()`
4. `COUNT()`

The answers for the preceding review questions are as follows:

Q1 - 1

Q2 - 3

Q3 - 2

Q4 - 1

Q5 - 1

Index

A

advanced SOQL statements
about 45
date fields, querying with 57
date formats 54
date literals 54
escape sequences 53
FOR REFERENCE clause 60
FOR VIEW clause 60
GROUP BY CUBE clause 61
GROUP BY ROLLUP clause 59, 60
lookup relationship 45
master-detail relationship 45
multiselect picklist values, filtering 50
OFFSET clause 62
relationship queries 45, 46
alias notation
about 25
usage 25, 27
AND operator
using 39
Apex Data Loader tool
about 97
downloading 99, 100
downloading, without Salesforce.com login 100
installing 101
operations 97
starting 101-103
system requisites 98

B

basic SOQL statements
alias notation 25-27
comparison operators 29
EXCLUDES operator 43
INCLUDES operator 43
IN operator 37
logical operators 39
ORDER BY clause 41
WHERE clause 27, 28

C

comparison operators
about 29
equals operator 30
greater than operator 34
greater than or equal to operator 33
less than operator 32
less than or equal to operator 32
LIKE operator 36
not equals operator 30
COUNT_DISTINCT() method
about 70
using 70, 71
COUNT(Field_Name) method
using 69, 70
COUNT() method
about 68
using 68
COUNT() query
limitations 82

D

Dataloader.io
about 93
using 93-96
date fields
querying with 57

date formats 54
date literals 54

E

equals operator
  using 30
escape sequences 53
EXCLUDES operator 43, 52, 53

F

Force.com Explorer software
  about 85
  installing 85-89
  using 85
FOR REFERENCE clause
  using 60
FOR VIEW clause
  using 60
functions, SOQL. *See* **SOQL functions**

G

greater than operator
  using 34, 35
greater than or equal to operator
  using 33, 34
GROUP BY clause
  about 67
  using 67, 68
GROUP BY CUBE clause
  using 61
GROUP BY ROLLUP clause
  using 59, 60

H

HAVING clause
  using 74, 75

I

INCLUDES operator 43, 50, 51
IN operator
  NOT IN operator 37
  using 37

L

less than operator
  using 32, 33
less than or equal to operator
  using 32
LIKE operator
  using 36
limitations, SOQL
  COUNT() query 82
  Governor limits 80
  Notes and Attachments objects 83
  OFFSET clause 82
  ORDER BY query 81
  relationship queries 82
  toLabel() query 81
logical operators
  about 39
  AND operator 39
  OR operator 39, 40

M

MAX() method
  about 72
  using 72, 73
MIN() method
  about 71, 72
  using 71
multiselect picklist values
  EXCLUDES operator 52
  filtering 50
  INCLUDES operator 50, 51

N

not equals operator
  using 30
Notes and Attachments objects
  limitations 83
NOT IN operator
  about 37
  using 37

O

objects
  limitations 79

OFFSET clause
limitations 82
using 62
operations, Apex Data Loader
delete 98
export 98
export all 98
hard delete 98
insert 97
update 97
upsert 97
ORDER BY clause
using 41, 42
ORDER BY query
limitations 81
OR operator
using 39-41

R

relationship queries
about 45-47
Child Relationship Name option 47-49
limitations 82
review questions 105

S

Salesforce Object Query Language. *See* **SOQL**
Salesforce Object Search Language (SOSL) 89
SOQL
about 5, 6
best practices 78, 79
limitations 80
limitations, in objects 79
purpose 8
standards 77, 78
syntax 9-12
using 6-8
SOQL functions
about 65
COUNT_DISTINCT() method 70
COUNT(Field_Name) method 69
COUNT() method 68
GROUP BY clause 67
HAVING clause 74, 75
MAX() method 72
MIN() method 71
SUM() method 73
toLabel() method 65
SOQL statement
writing 13-23
Structured Query Language (SQL) 5
SUM() method
using 73

T

toLabel() method
about 65
using 65, 66
toLabel() query
limitations 81

W

WHERE clause
about 27
usage 28, 29
Workbench
about 89
installing 89-92

About Packt Publishing

Packt, pronounced 'packed', published its first book "*Mastering phpMyAdmin for Effective MySQL Management*" in April 2004 and subsequently continued to specialize in publishing highly focused books on specific technologies and solutions.

Our books and publications share the experiences of your fellow IT professionals in adapting and customizing today's systems, applications, and frameworks. Our solution based books give you the knowledge and power to customize the software and technologies you're using to get the job done. Packt books are more specific and less general than the IT books you have seen in the past. Our unique business model allows us to bring you more focused information, giving you more of what you need to know, and less of what you don't.

Packt is a modern, yet unique publishing company, which focuses on producing quality, cutting-edge books for communities of developers, administrators, and newbies alike. For more information, please visit our website: `www.packtpub.com`.

About Packt Open Source

In 2010, Packt launched two new brands, Packt Open Source and Packt Enterprise, in order to continue its focus on specialization. This book is part of the Packt Open Source brand, home to books published on software built around Open Source licences, and offering information to anybody from advanced developers to budding web designers. The Open Source brand also runs Packt's Open Source Royalty Scheme, by which Packt gives a royalty to each Open Source project about whose software a book is sold.

Writing for Packt

We welcome all inquiries from people who are interested in authoring. Book proposals should be sent to `author@packtpub.com`. If your book idea is still at an early stage and you would like to discuss it first before writing a formal book proposal, contact us; one of our commissioning editors will get in touch with you.

We're not just looking for published authors; if you have strong technical skills but no writing experience, our experienced editors can help you develop a writing career, or simply get some additional reward for your expertise.

[PACKT] open source
community experience distilled
PUBLISHING

Microsoft SQL Server 2012 with Hadoop

ISBN: 978-1-78217-798-2 Paperback: 96 pages

Integrate data between Apache Hadoop and SQL Server 2012 and provide business intelligence on the heterogeneous data

1. Integrate data from unstructured (Hadoop) and structured (SQL Server 2012) sources.
2. Configure and install connectors for a bi-directional transfer of data.
3. Full of illustrations, diagrams, and tips with clear, step-by-step instructions and practical examples.

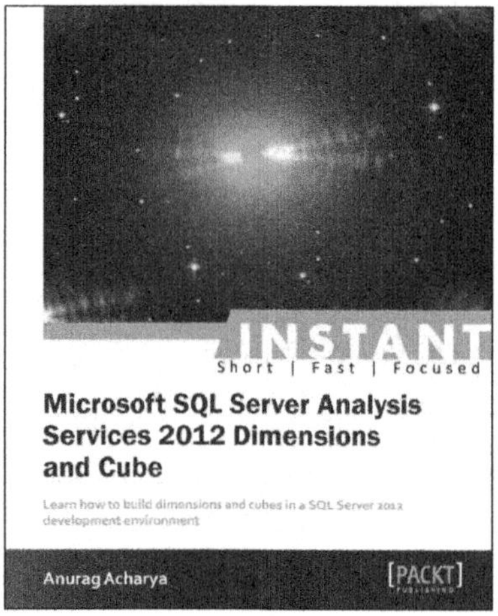

Instant Microsoft SQL Server Analysis Services 2012 Dimensions and Cube

ISBN: 978-1-84968-872-7 Paperback: 72 pages

Learn how to build dimensions and cubes in a SQL Server 2012 development environment

1. Learn something new in an Instant! A short, fast, focused guide delivering immediate results.
2. Create your own SQL Server development environment.
3. Full of practical tutorials on cube design and development.
4. Learn how to efficiently administrate and manage your SQL Server instance.

Please check **www.PacktPub.com** for information on our titles

Made in the USA
Columbia, SC
23 June 2020

12215676R00072